Internet
in an Hour
for Managers

Chris Katsaropoulos
Don Mayo
Kathy Berkemeyer

Acknowledgements

To my mother, Mary Katsaropoulos, for encouraging my writing endeavors. A special thanks to Jennifer Frew, Peter McCarthy, and John Visaggi at DDC Publishing for always listening and knowing the right thing to do.

Chris Katsaropoulos

To Jen for her double-duty efforts as Major Domo of the sanity patrol, Lisa Miller for always being available to help and laugh, and Marivel for her unconditional encouragement.
Don Mayo

Dedicated to the memory of my parents, John and Gert Madden.

Kathy Berkemeyer

Managing Editor	Technical Editors	English Editors	Illustrations	Design and Layout
Jennifer Frew	Monique Peterson	Jennifer Frew	Ryan Sather	Elsa Johannesson
	Cathy Vesecky	Monique Peterson		Midori Nakamura
				Paul Wray

ISBN: 1-56243-602-3
Cat. No. HR2
First DDC Publishing, Inc. Printing:
10 9 8 7 6 5 4 3 2 1
Printed in the United States of America.

Contents

Contents

Introduction

This Book is Designed for You . . .

if you are a busy manager, executive, staff member, or small business owner who wants to find out how to get things done using the Internet.

The Internet and especially the World Wide Web provide a vast and ever-growing resource where you can find information and business tools to help you be more effective on the job. This book shows you where and how to find the best resources available.

This book has two main sections, Internet Basics and Web Resources.

Internet Basics

In Internet Basics, you can learn how to:

- Use Netscape Navigator to browse the World Wide.
- Send and receive e-mail messages with Netscape Messenger.
- Use Internet Explorer to browse the World Wide Web.
- Send and receive e-mail messages with Microsoft Outlook Express.
- Access the Internet using America Online.
- Send and receive e-mail messages with America Online.
- Find information on the Web with search engines.

Web Resources

Web Resources shows you ways you can use the Web to do your job more effectively.

Web Resources is organized by general categories (Finding News and Information, Finance and Economics, Operations, Laws and Regulatons, Sales and Marketing), then by topics (such as Find Business Capital and Plan and Book Travel Online).

Each topic showcases top Web sites that offer practical business resources. Each Web site listing provides you with the site's URL (Web address) and a brief description of how the site can help you. In many cases an illustration of the Web site is also provided.

Appendices

Three appendices give you additional reference information about the following topics:

Essential Downloads
A listing of Web sites where you can download useful software, much of it available free of charge or for a minimal registration fee.

Timesaving Tools
Use these sites to get quick answers and information.

Viruses
An overview of what computers viruses can do to your computer and how to avoid them.

What Do I Need to Use This Book

This book assumes that you have some general knowledge and experience with computers and that you already know how to perform the following tasks:

- Use a mouse (double-click, etc.).
- Make your way around Microsoft Windows 95.
- Install and run programs.

If you are completely new to computers as well as the World Wide Web, you may want to refer to DDC's **Learning Microsoft Windows 95** or **Learning the Internet**.

This book also assumes that you have access to browser applications such as Microsoft Internet Explorer 4.0, Netscape Navigator 4.0, or America Online.

> √ *If you do not currently have these applications, contact your Internet Service Provider for instructions on how to download them. You can also use other browsers or previous versions such as Explorer 3.0 and Navigator 3.0 to browse the Web.*

You must have an Internet connection, either through your school, your office, or an online service such as America Online or CompuServe. How to get connected to the Internet is not covered in this book.

Please read over the following list of "must haves" to ensure that you are ready to be connected to the Internet.

- A computer (with a recommended minimum of 16 MB of RAM) and a modem port.

- A modem (with a recommended minimum speed of 14.4kbps, and suggested speed of 28.8kbps) that is connected to an analog phone line (assuming you are not using a direct Internet connection through a school, corporation, etc.).
- Established access to the Internet through an online service, independent Internet service provider, etc.
- A great deal of patience. The Internet is a fun and exciting place. But getting connected can be frustrating at times. Expect to run into occasional glitches, to get disconnected from time to time, and to experience occasional difficulty in viewing certain Web pages or features. The more up-to-date your equipment and software are, however, the less difficulty you will probably experience.

Internet Cautions

ACCURACY: Be cautious not to believe everything on the Internet. Almost anyone can publish information on the Internet, and since there is no Internet editor or monitor, some information may be false. All information found on the World Wide Web should be checked for accuracy through additional reputable sources.

SECURITY: When sending information over the Internet, be prepared to let the world have access to it. Computer hackers can find ways to access anything that you send to anyone over the Internet, including e-mail. Be cautious when sending confidential information to anyone.

VIRUSES: These small, usually destructive computer programs hide inside of innocent-looking programs. Once a virus is executed, it attaches itself to other programs. When triggered, often by the occurrence of a date or time on the computer's internal clock/calendar, it executes a nuisance or damaging function, such as displaying a message on your screen, corrupting your files, or reformatting your hard disk.

B
A
S
I
C
S

Netscape Navigator: 1

◆ **About Netscape Navigator** ◆ **Start Netscape Navigator**
◆ **The Netscape Screen** ◆ **Exit Netscape Navigator**

About Netscape Navigator

■ Netscape Navigator 4.0 is the Internet browser component of Netscape Communicator, a set of integrated tools for browsing the World Wide Web, finding and downloading information, shopping for and purchasing goods and services, creating Web pages, and communicating with others with e-mail. This chapter focuses on the Netscape Navigator browser. Netscape Messenger, the e-mail component, is covered in Chapters 4-6.

Start Netscape Navigator

To start Netscape Navigator (Windows 95):

• Click the Start button ![Start].

• Click Programs, Netscape Communicator, Netscape Navigator.

   OR

• If you have a shortcut to Netscape Communicator ![Netscape Communicator] on your desktop, double-click it to start Netscape Navigator.

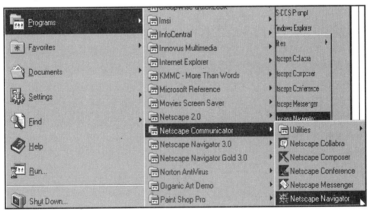

√ *The first time you start Netscape Communicator, the New Profile Setup dialog box appears. Enter information about your e-mail name and service provider in the dialog boxes that appear. If you do not know the information, you can leave it blank until you are ready to fill it in.*

2

The Netscape Screen

- The Netscape Navigator screen contains features that will be very helpful as you explore the Internet. Some of these features are constant and some change depending on the Web site visited or the task attempted or completed.

    √ *To gain more space on screen, you may want to hide toolbars and the Location line. Go to the View menu and select the desired hide/show options.*

Title bar Displays the name of the program (Netscape) and the current Web page (Welcome to Netscape). Note the standard Windows minimize, maximize/restore, and close buttons at the right.

Menu bar Displays menus, which provide drop-down lists of commands for executing Netscape tasks.

Navigation toolbar Contains buttons for moving between and printing Web pages. The name and icon on each button identify the command for the button. You can access these commands quickly and easily by clicking the mouse on the desired button.

If the toolbar buttons are not visible, open the View menu and click Show Navigation Toolbar.

Location toolbar Displays the electronic address of the currently displayed Web page in the Location field. You can also type the electronic address of a Web page in the Location field and press Enter to access it. A Web site address is called a Uniform Resource Locator (URL).

If the Location toolbar is not visible, open the View menu and click Show Location Toolbar.

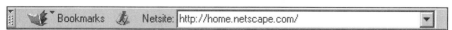

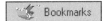

The Location toolbar also contains the Bookmarks QuickFile button. Click this button to view a list of sites that you have bookmarked for quick access. (For more information on bookmarks, see "Netscape Navigator: 3" on page 9.)

The Location button is also located on this toolbar. The word *Netsite* displays if the current Web site uses Netscape software. The word *Location* replaces Netsite if the site does not use Netscape as its primary software.

Personal toolbar

Contains buttons or links that you add to connect to your favorite sites. When you install Netscape Communicator, the Internet, Lookup, New&Cool, and Netcaster buttons are on the Personal toolbar by default. You can delete these buttons and add your own by displaying the desired Web site and dragging the Location icon onto the Personal toolbar.

Netscape's status indicator

Netscape's icon pulses when Netscape is processing a request (command) that you enter. To return immediately to Netscape's home page, click on this icon.

Status bar

When a Web page is opening, the Status bar indicates progress by a percentage displayed in the center and the security level of the page being loaded by a lock in the far-left corner. When you place the cursor over a hyperlink, the Status bar displays the URL of the link.

Component toolbar

The buttons on this toolbar are links to other Communicator components: Navigator, (Messenger) Mailbox, (Collabra) Discussions, and (Page) Composer.

Exit Netscape Navigator

■ Exiting Netscape Navigator and disconnecting from your Internet Service Provider (ISP) are two separate steps. You can actually disconnect from your service provider and still have Netscape Navigator open. (Remember that you must first establish a connection to the Internet via your ISP to use Netscape to access information on the Web.) You can also disconnect from Navigator and still have your ISP open.

■ There are times when you may want to keep Netscape open to read information obtained from the Web, access information stored on your hard disk using Netscape, or to compose e-mail to send later. If you don't disconnect from your ISP and you pay an hourly rate, you will continue incurring charges.

> **CAUTION** When you exit Netscape, you do not necessarily exit from your Internet service provider. Be sure to check the disconnect procedure from your ISP so that you will not continue to be charged for time online. Most services disconnect when a certain amount of time passes with no activity.

√ *Once you disconnect from your ISP, you can no longer access new Web information. Remember: Netscape Navigator is a browser; it is not an Internet connection.*

√ *You can disconnect from your ISP and view Web information accessed during the current session using the Back and Forward toolbar buttons. This is because the visited sites are stored in the memory of your computer. However, Web sites visited during the current session are erased from your computer memory when you exit Netscape.*

◆ **The Navigation Toolbar**

◆ **URLs (Uniform Resource Locator)** ◆ **Open World Wide Web Sites**

The Navigation Toolbar

- The Netscape Navigation toolbar displays buttons for Netscape's most commonly used commands. Note that each button contains an icon and a word describing the button's function. Choosing any of these buttons activates the indicated task immediately.

- If the Navigation toolbar is not visible, select Show <u>N</u>avigation Toolbar from the <u>V</u>iew menu.

 Moves back through pages previously displayed. Back is available only if you have moved around among Web pages in the current Navigator session; otherwise, it is dimmed.

 Moves forward through pages previously displayed. Forward is available only if you have used the Back button; otherwise, it is dimmed.

 Reloads the currently displayed Web page. Use this button if the current page is taking too long to display or to update the current page with any changes that may have been made since the page was downloaded.

 Displays the home page.

 Displays Netscape's Net Search Page. You can select one of several search tools from this page.

 Displays a menu with helpful links to Internet sites that contain search tools and services.

 Prints the displayed page, topic, or article.

 Displays security information for the displayed Web page as well as information on Netscape security features.

Stops the loading of a Web page.

URLs (Uniform Resource Locator)

■ Every Web site has a unique address called its URL (Uniform Resource Locator). A URL has four parts:

Part	Example	Description
Protocol	**http://**	The protocol indicates the method used for communicating on the internet The most common is http:// , which stands for Hypertext Transfer Protocol. Another protocol—ftp:// (file transfer protocol)—is used with internet sites designed to make files available for uploading and downloading.
Address type	**www.**	www. stands for World Wide Web and indicates that the site is located on the Web. Occasionally, you may find other address types, but www. addresses are the most common.
Identifier of the site's owner	**ddcpub**	This part of the address identifies who is responsible for the Web site.
Domain	**.com, .gov, .org, .edu, etc.** (see below)	The domain indicates the kind of organization that sponsors the site (company, government, non-profit organization, educational institution, and so on).

■ For example, the DDC publishing URL breaks down as follows:

http://www.ddcpub.com

Hypertext Transfer Protocol   World Wide Web   Company name   Domain

■ There are seven common domains:

com	Commercial enterprise	**edu**	Educational institution
org	Non-commercial organization	**mil**	U. S. Military location
net	A network that has a gateway to the Internet	**gov**	Local, state, or federal government location
int	International organization		

Open World Wide Web Sites

■ There are several ways to access a Web site. If you know the site's address, you can enter the correct Web address (URL) on the Location field on the Location toolbar.

■ If the address you are entering is the address of a site you have visited recently or that you have bookmarked (see "Netscape Navigator: 3" on page 9 for more information on Bookmarks), you will notice as you begin to type the address that Netscape attempts to complete it for you. If the address that Netscape suggests is the one you want, press Enter.

■ If the address that Netscape suggests is not correct, keep typing to complete the desired address and then press Enter. Or, you can click the down arrow next to the Location field to view a list of other possible matches, select an address, and press Enter.

■ You can also enter the URL in the Open Page dialog box. To do so, select Open Page from the File menu, select Navigator, type the URL, and click Open.

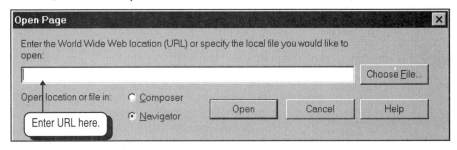

■ There are a couple of shortcuts for entering URL addresses. One shortcut involves omitting the http://www. prefix from the Web address. Netscape assumes the **http://** protocol and the **www** that indicates that the site is located on the Web. If you are trying to connect to a company Web site, entering the company name is generally sufficient. Netscape assumes the **.com** suffix. For example, entering **ddcpub** on the location line and pressing Enter would reach the **http://www.ddcpub.com** address.

   √ *Don't be discouraged if the connection to the World Wide Web site is not made immediately. The site may be off-line temporarily. The site may also be very busy with others users trying to access it. Be sure the URL is typed accurately. Occasionally, it takes several tries to connect to a site.*

◆ History List ◆ Bookmarks ◆ Add Bookmarks
◆ Delete Bookmarks ◆ Print Web Pages

History List

- While you move back and forth among Web sites, Netscape automatically records each of these site locations in a **history** list, which is temporarily stored on your computer. You can use the history list to track what sites you have already visited or to jump to a recently viewed site.

  √ *As you move from one site to another on the Web, you may find yourself asking, "How did I get here?" The History list is an easy way to see the path you followed to get to the current destination.*

- To view the history list, click <u>H</u>istory on the <u>C</u>ommunicator menu, or press Ctrl+H. To link to a site shown in the history list, double-click on it.

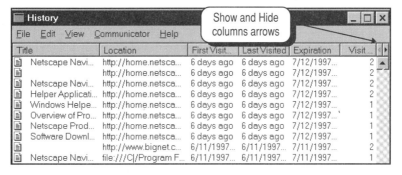

Bookmarks

- A **bookmark** is a placeholder containing the title and URL of a Web page that, when selected, links directly to that page. If you find a Web site that you like and want to revisit, you can create a bookmark to record its location. (See "Add Bookmarks" on page 10.) The Netscape bookmark feature maintains permanent records of the Web sites in your bookmark files so that you can return to them easily.

- You can view the Bookmarks menu by selecting Bookmarks from the Communicator menu or by clicking on the Bookmarks QuickFile button 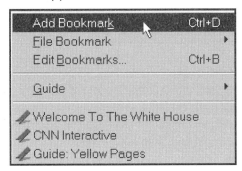 on the Location toolbar. The drop-down menu shown below appears.

Add Bookmark	Ctrl+D
File Bookmark	▶
Edit Bookmarks...	Ctrl+B
Guide	▶
Welcome To The White House	
CNN Interactive	
Guide: Yellow Pages	

Add Bookmarks

- Display the Web page to add, go to Bookmarks on the Communicator menu and click Add Bookmark.

Netscape does not confirm that a bookmark has been added to the file.

- You can create bookmarks from addresses in the History folder. Click Communicator, History and select the listing to bookmark. Right-click on it and choose Add To Bookmarks from the menu.

Delete Bookmarks

- Bookmarks may be deleted at anytime. For example, you may wish to delete a bookmark if a Web site no longer exists or remove one that is no longer of interest to you.
- To delete a bookmark do the following:
  - Click Communicator.
  - Click Bookmarks.
  - Click Edit Bookmarks.
  - In the Bookmarks window, select the bookmark you want to delete by clicking on it from the bookmark list.
  - Press the Delete key.

OR

- Right-click on the bookmark and select <u>D</u>elete Bookmark from the drop-down menu.

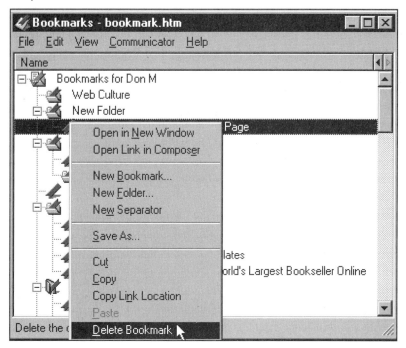

Print Web Pages

- One of the many uses of the Internet is to print out information. You can print a page as it appears on screen, or you can print it as plain text. Only displayed pages can be printed.
- To print a Web page, display it and do the following:

  - Click the Print button on the Navigation toolbar.

    OR

  - Click <u>P</u>rint on the <u>F</u>ile menu.
  - In the Print dialog box that displays, select the desired print options and click Print.
- In most cases, the Web page will be printed in the format shown in the Web page display.

Netscape Messenger: 4

◆ Configure Netscape Mail ◆ Start Netscape Messenger
◆ The Message List Window ◆ Get New Mail ◆ Read Messages
◆ Delete a Message ◆ Print Messages ◆ Bookmark a Message

Configure Netscape Mail

√ *This section assumes that you have already set up an e-mail account with a service provider. If you do not have an e-mail address, contact your Internet Service Provider. Establishing a modem connection and configuring your computer to send and receive mail can be frustrating. Don't be discouraged; what follows are steps that will get you connected, but some of the information may have to be supplied by your Internet Service Provider. Calling for help will save you time and frustration.*

■ The Netscape Communicator browser suite includes a comprehensive e-mail program called Netscape Messenger, which allows you to send, receive, save, and print e-mail messages and attachments.

■ Before you can use Messenger to send and receive e-mail, you must configure the program with your e-mail account information (user name, e-mail address, and mail server names). You may have already filled in this information if you completed the New Profile Setup Wizard when you installed Netscape Communicator.

■ You may have configured Netscape Messenger to receive and send e-mail messages when you first installed the program. If not, follow these steps to get connected. You can also use these steps to update and change settings to your e-mail account.

Identity Settings

• Open the Edit menu on the Netscape Navigator or Netscape Messenger menu and select Preferences. Click Identity in the Mail & Groups Category list to and do the following:

Enter your name and e-mail address in the first two boxes. Enter any other optional information in the Identity dialog box.

12

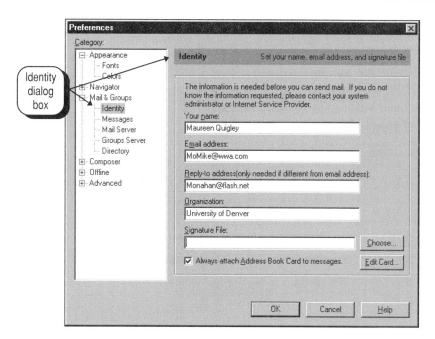

Mail Server Preference Settings

- Click Mail Server to configure your mailbox so that you can send and receive mail.

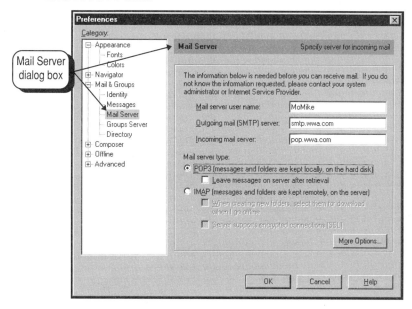

- Enter mail server user name in the first box. This is usually the part of your e-mail address that appears in front of the @ sign.

- Enter your outgoing and incoming mail server. Check with your Internet Service Provider if you are not sure what these settings are.

- Click OK to save and close the Preference settings. You should now be able to send and receive e-mail messages and/or files.

Start Netscape Messenger

■ To start Netscape Messenger:

- Click the Mailbox icon  on the Component bar.
  OR
- Start the Netscape Messenger program from the Netscape Communicator submenu on the Start menu.

🔲 KMMC - More Than Words ▶	💬 Netscape Collabra	
🔲 Microsoft Reference ▶	🖊 Netscape Composer	
🔲 Movies Screen Saver ▶	📠 Netscape Conference	
🔲 Netscape 2.0 ▶	✦ Netscape Messenger	
🔲 Netscape Communicator ▶	🖧 Netscape Navigator	

The Message List Window

■ After you launch Messenger, a message list window will open, displaying the contents of the e-mail Inbox folder. You can retrieve, read, forward, and reply to messages from this window.

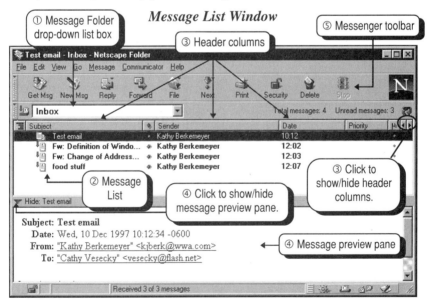

Message List Window

14

- The message list window includes the following:

① The **Message Folder drop-down list box** displays the currently selected message folder, the contents of which are displayed in the message list below the drop-down box. Click the down arrow to display a list of other message folders. Select a different folder from the list to display its contents in the message list area.

② The **message list** displays a header for each of the messages contained in the currently selected message folder (Inbox is the default).

③ **Header columns** list the categories of information available for each message, such as subject, sender, and date. You can customize the display of the header columns in a number of ways:

- Resize column widths by placing the mouse pointer over the right border of a column until the pointer changes to a double arrow, and then click and drag the border to the desired size.

- Rearrange the order of the columns by clicking and dragging a header to a new location in the series.

- Show/hide different columns by clicking the arrow buttons on the upper-right side of the message list window.

   √ *If text in a message header is cut off so that you cannot read it all, position the mouse pointer on the header in the column containing the cropped text. A small box will display the complete text for that column of the header, as in the example below:*

④ The **message preview pane** displays the content of the message currently selected from the message list. You can show/hide the preview pane by clicking on the blue triangle icon in the bottom-left corner of the message list pane. You can resize the preview pane or the message list pane by placing the pointer over the border between the two panes until the pointer changes to a double arrow and then dragging the border up or down to the desired size.

⑤ The **Messenger toolbar** displays buttons for activating Netscape Messenger's most commonly used commands. Note that each button contains an image and a word describing the function. Choosing any of these buttons will activate the indicated task immediately.

Messenger Toolbar Buttons and Functions

 Retrieves new mail from your Internet mail server and loads it into the Inbox message folder.

 Opens the Message Composition screen allowing you to compose new mail messages.

 Allows you to reply to the sender of an e-mail message or to the sender and all other recipients of the e-mail message.

 Forwards a message you have received to another address.

 Stores the current message in one of six Messenger default file folders or in a new folder that you create.

 Selects and displays the next of the unread messages in your Inbox.

 Prints the displayed message.

 Displays the security status of a message.

 Deletes the selected message. Deleted messages are moved to the Trash folder. You must delete contents of Trash folder to remove messages from your computer.

Get New Mail

- Since new e-mail messages are stored on a remote ISP mail server, you must be connected to the Internet to access them. To retrieve new messages to your computer, click the Get Msg button

 on the Messenger toolbar.

- In the Password Entry dialog box that follows, enter your e-mail password in the blank text box and click OK. (If you do not know your e-mail password, contact your ISP.)

√ *Messenger saves your password for the rest of the current Messenger session. You must re-enter it each time you retrieve new mail, unless you set Messenger to save your password permanently. To do so:*

- Click Edit, Preferences.
- Click once on Mail Server under Mail & Groups.
- Click the More Options button.
- Select the Remember my mail password check box and click OK twice.

■ The Getting New Messages box opens, displaying the status of your message retrieval.

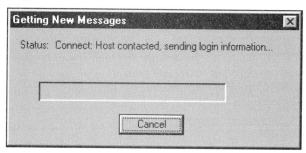

■ Once your new messages are retrieved, they are listed in the message list window. By default, Messenger stores new mail messages in the Inbox folder.

Read Messages

■ You can read a message in the preview pane of the message list window or in a separate window.

■ To read a message in the preview pane, click on the desired message header in the message list. If the message does not appear, click on the blue triangle icon at the bottom of the message list window to display the preview pane.

■ To open and read a message in a separate window, double-click on the desired message header in the message list. You can close a message after reading it by clicking File, Close or by clicking on the Close button (X) in the upper-right corner of the window.

■ To read the next unread message, click the Next button ⬚ on the Messenger toolbar. Or, if you have reached the end of the current message, you can press the spacebar to proceed to the next unread message.

- Once you have read a message, it remains stored in the Inbox folder until you delete it or file it in another folder. (See "Delete a Message" below.)

  √ *You do not have to be online to read e-mail. You can reduce your online charges if you disconnect from your ISP after retrieving your messages and read them offline.*

  √ *Icons located to the left of message headers in the message list identify each message as either unread* ✉ *(retrieved during a previous Messenger session), new* ✉ *(and unread), or read* ✉.

Delete a Message

- To delete a message, select its header from the message list

  window and click the Delete button [Delete] in the Messenger toolbar.

  √ *To select more than one message to delete, click the Ctrl button while you click each message header.*

Print Messages

- In order to print a message you must first display the message in either the preview pane of the message list window or in a separate window, then:

  • Click the Print button [Print] on the Messenger toolbar.

  • In the Print dialog box that appears, select the desired print options and click OK.

Print Dialog Box

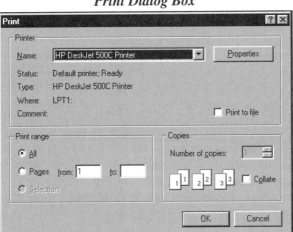

Bookmark a Message

- You can add an e-mail message to your Bookmarks folder for easy access from anywhere within the Communicator suite. To bookmark a message:

  - Display the message you want to bookmark in either the preview pane of the message list window or in a separate window.

  - Select Communicator, Bookmarks, Add Bookmark.

- Messenger will add the message to the bottom of your Bookmarks menu.

◆ **Compose New Messages** ◆ **Send Messages**
◆ **The Message Composition Toolbar** ◆ **Reply to Mail**
◆ **Forward Mail** ◆ **Add Entries to the Personal Address Book**
◆ **Address a New Message Using the Personal Address Book**

Compose New Messages

- You can compose an e-mail message in Netscape Messenger while you are connected to the Internet, or while you are offline. When composing an e-mail message online, you can send the message immediately after creating it. When composing a message offline (which is considered proper Netiquette—net etiquette), you will need to store the message in your Unsent Messages folder until you are online and can send it.

- To create a message, you first need to open Messenger's Message Composition window. To do so:

    - Click the New Message button New Msg.
        √ *The Message Composition window displays.*

Netscape Message Composition Window

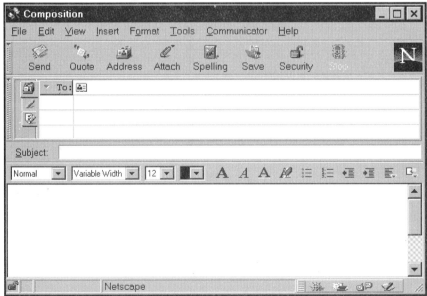

√ *You can hide any toolbar in the Message Composition screen by going to View, Hide Message Toolbar or Hide Formatting Toolbar.*

√ *If you do not know the recipient's address, you can look it up and insert it from your personal address book (see page 24) or an online directory.*

■ In the Message Composition window, type the Internet address(es) of the message recipient(s) in the To: field. Or, click the Address button **Address** on the Message Composition toolbar and select an address to insert (see pages 24-26 for more information on using the Address Book).

√ *If you are sending the message to multiple recipients, press Enter after typing each recipient's address.*

■ After inserting the address(es), click the To: icon **To:** to display a drop-down menu of other addressee options. Select any of the following options from the drop-down menu and enter the recipient information indicated.

To	The e-mail address of the person to whom the message is being sent.
CC (Carbon Copy)	The e-mail addresses of people who will receive copies of the message.
BCC (Blind Carbon Copy)	Same as CC, except these names will not appear anywhere in the message, so other recipients will not know that the person(s) listed in the BCC field received a copy.
Group	Names of newsgroups that will receive this message (similar to Mail To).
Reply To	The e-mail address where replies should be sent.
Follow-up To	Another newsgroup heading; used to identify newsgroups to which comments should be posted (similar to Reply To).

■ Click in the Subject field (or press Tab to move the cursor there) and type the subject of the message.

■ Click in the blank composition area below the Subject field and type the body of your message. Word wrap occurs automatically, and you can cut and paste quotes from other messages or text from other programs. You can also check the spelling of your message by clicking on the Spelling button  on the Message Composition toolbar and responding to the dialog prompts that follow.

Send Messages

- Once you have created a message, you have three choices:
  - to send the message immediately
  - to store the message in the Unsent Messages folder to be sent later (File, Send Later)
  - to save the message in the Drafts folder to be finished and sent later (File, Save Draft)

To send a message immediately:

- Click the Send button [Send] on the Message Composition toolbar.

The Message Composition Toolbar

- The toolbar in the Message Composition window has several features that are specific only to this screen.
- Notice that the main toolbar buttons contain a task name and illustration.

Message Composition Toolbar

	Immediately sends current message.
	Used when replying to a message, the Quote feature allows you to include text from the original message.
	Select an address from the addresses stored in your personal address book to insert into address fields.
	By clicking the Attach button, you can send a file, a Web page, or your personal address card along with your e-mail message.
	Checks for spelling errors in the current message.

22

Lets you save your message as a draft for later use.

 Sets the security status of a message.

 Stops the display of an HTML message or a message with an HTML attachment.

- The Formatting toolbar provides commands for applying styles, fonts, font size, bulleted lists, and inserting objects.

Reply to Mail

- To reply to a message, select or open the message to reply to and click the Reply button ⬚.

- From the submenu that appears, select Reply to Sender to reply to the original sender only, or select Reply to Sender and All Recipients to send a reply to the sender and all other recipients of the original message. Selecting one of these options lets you reply to the message without having to enter the recipient's name or e-mail address.

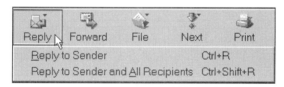

√ The Message Composition window opens, with the To, Cc, and Subject fields filled in for you.

- Compose your reply as you would a new message.

- To include a copy of the original message with your reply, click the Quote button ⬚ on the Message Composition toolbar. You can edit the original message and header text as you wish.

- When you are finished, click the Send button ⬚ to send the message immediately.

Forward Mail

■ To forward a message automatically without having to enter the recipient's name or e-mail address, first select or open the message to forward. Then click on the Forward button .

   The Message Composition window opens, with the Subject field filled in for you.

Subject:	[Fwd: Andy's Birthday Party]

■ Type the e-mail address of the new recipient in the To field, or click the Address button ⊡Address⊡ on the Message Composition toolbar and select a name from your Address Book (see "Address a New Message Using the Personal Address Book" on page 26 for information on using the Address Book).

■ If the original message does not appear in the composition area, click the Quote button ⊡Quote⊡ on the Message Composition toolbar to insert it.

■ Click in the composition area and edit the message as desired. You can also type any additional text you want to include with the forwarded message.

■ When you are done, click the Send button ⊡Send⊡ to send the message immediately. Or, select Send Later from the File menu to store the message in the Unsent Messages mailbox to be sent later. To save the reply as a draft to be edited and sent later, select Save Draft from the File menu.

Add Entries to the Personal Address Book

■ You can compile a personal address book to store e-mail addresses and other information about your most common e-mail recipients. You can then use the address book to find and automatically insert an address when creating a new message.

■ To add a name to the address book:

   • Select Address Book from the Communicator menu. The Address Book window displays.

24

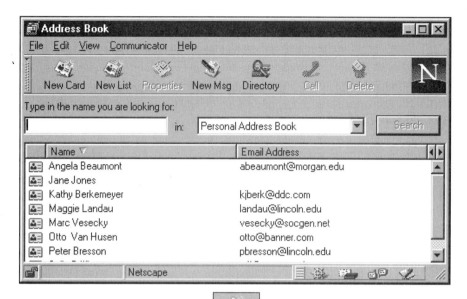

- Click the New Card button 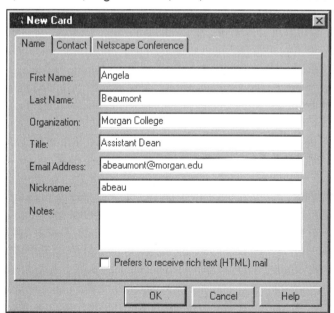 on the Address Book toolbar.
- In the New Card box that appears, enter the recipient's first name, last name, organization, title, and e-mail address.

- In the Nickname field, type a nickname for the recipient, if desired (the nickname must be unique among the entries in your address book). When addressing a message, you can use the recipient's nickname in the To field, rather than typing the entire address, and Messenger will automatically fill in the full e-mail address.

- In the Notes field, type any notes you want to store about the recipient.

- Click the Contact tab, if desired, and enter the recipient's postal address and phone number.

- Click OK.

■ You can edit an address book entry at any time by double-clicking on the person's name in the Address Book window.

■ You can automatically add the name and address of the sender of a message you are reading by selecting Add to Address Book from the Message menu and selecting Sender from the submenu. The New Card dialog box opens, with the First Name, Last Name, and E-mail Address fields filled in for you. You can enter a nickname for the person, if desired, and any other information you want in the remaining fields.

Address a New Message Using the Personal Address Book

■ To insert an address from your address book into a new message:

- Click the New Msg button New Msg to open the Message Composition window.

- Click on the Address button Address on the Message Composition toolbar and select a recipient(s) from the list in the Address Book window. Drag the selected name(s) into the To field in the Message Composition window. Click the Close button X in the Address Book window when you are finished.

OR

- Begin typing the name or nickname of the recipient in the To field of the Message Composition window. If the name is included in the Address Book, Messenger will recognize it and finish entering the name and address for you.

Netscape Messenger: 6

◆ Attached Files ◆ View File Attachments
◆ Save Attached Files ◆ Attach Files to Messages

Attached Files

■ Sometimes an e-mail message will come with a separate file(s) attached. Messages containing attachments are indicated when you display a message and it contains a paperclip icon ⬚ to the right of the message header. Attachment can be used, for example, when you want to send someone an Excel spreadsheet or a video clip.

■ With Messenger, you can view both plain text attachments and binary attachments. **Binary** files are files containing more than plain text (i.e., images, sound clips, and formatted text, such as spreadsheets and word processor documents).

■ Almost any e-mail program can read plain text files. Binary files, however, must be decoded by the receiving e-mail program before they can be displayed in readable form. This requires that the e-mail software have the capability to decode either MIME (Multi-Purpose Internet Mail Extension) or UUEncode protocol. Messenger can decode both. When a binary attachment arrives, Messenger automatically recognizes and decodes it.

View File Attachments

■ File or HTML attachments are displayed in one of two ways.

• If you select View, Attachments, Inline, you see the attachment appended to the body of the message in a separate attachment window below the message. Essentially there is a series of sequential windows—one with the message and the other with the attachment.

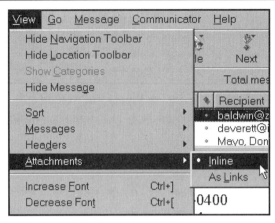

√ *Only plain text, images, and Web page attachments can be viewed inline.*

- If the attachment is HTML code, you will see a fully formatted Web page.

- If you select View, Attachments, As Links, the attachment window displays an attachment box displaying the details of the attachment. It also serves as a link to the attachment.

√ *Viewing attachments as links reduces the time it takes to open a message on screen.*

- Clicking on the blue-highlighted text in the attachment box will display the attachment.

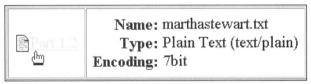

- You can right-click on the attachment icon box to display a menu of mail options such as forwarding, replying, or deleting the message.

  - By right-clicking on the actual attachment, you can choose from several file save options, such as saving the image or file in a separate file on your hard drive, as Windows wallpaper, or saving the image and putting a shortcut to the image on your desktop.

  - If you open a Web page attachment while online, you will find that the Web page serves as an actual connection to the Web site and that all links on the page are active. If you are not connected, the Web page will display fully formatted, but it will not be active.

- If an attached image displays as a link even after you select View, Attachments, Inline, it is probably because it is an image type that Messenger does not recognize. In this case, you need to install and/or open a plug-in or program with which to view the unrecognized image.

■ If you know you have the appropriate application or plug-in installed, click the Save File button in the Unknown File Type dialog box and save the attachment to your hard drive or disk (see "Save Attached Files" below). Then start the necessary application or plug-in and open the saved attachment file to view it.

■ If you do not have the necessary application or plug-in, click on the More Info button in the Unknown File Type dialog box. The Netscape Plug-in Finder Web page opens, displaying some general information about plug-ins, a list of plug-ins that will open the selected attachment, and hyperlinks to Web sites where you can download the given plug-ins.

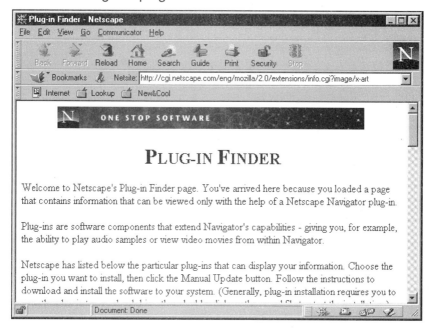

Save Attached Files

■ You can save an attached file to your hard drive or disk for future use or reference. To save an attachment:

• Open the message containing the attachment to save.

• If the attachment is in inline view, convert it to a link (View, Attachments, As Links).

• Right-click on the link and select Save Link As.

OR

- Click on the link to open the attachment. Select File, Save As, or, if Messenger does not recognize the attachment's file type, click the Save File button in the Unknown File Type dialog box.

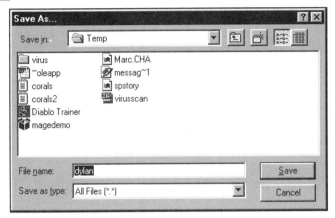

- In the Save As dialog box that follows, click the Save in drop-down list box and select the drive and folder(s) in which to save the file.
- Click in the File name text box and type a name for the file.
- Click Save.

Attach Files to Messages

- With Messenger, you can attach both plain text and binary files (images, media clips, formatted text documents, etc.) to e-mail messages. You may wish to check if your recipient's e-mail software can decode MIME or UUEncode protocols. Otherwise, binary attachments will not open and display properly on the recipient's computer.

- To attach a file to an e-mail message:

  - Click the Attach button [Attach] on the Message Composition toolbar, and select File from the drop-down menu that appears.

  - In the Enter file to attach dialog box that follows, click the Look in drop-down list box and select the drive and folder containing the file to attach.

  - Then select the file to attach and click Open.

- After you have attached a file, the Attachments field in the Mail Composition window displays the name and location of the attached file.

  √ *Messages containing attachments usually take longer to send than those without attachments. When attaching very large files or multiple files, you may want to zip (compress) the files before attaching them. To do so, both you and the recipient need a file compression program, such as WinZip or PKZip.*

Attach Files and Documents

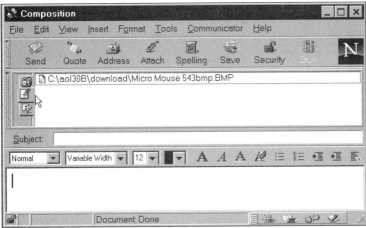

- Once you have attached the desired files and finished composing your message, you can send the e-mail, save it in the Unsent Messages folder for later delivery, or save it as a draft for later editing.

◆ **Start Internet Explorer 4**

◆ **Internet Explorer Screen** ◆ **Exit Internet Explorer**

Start Internet Explorer 4

■ When you first install Internet Explorer and you are using the Active Desktop, you may see the message illustrated below when you turn on your computer. If you are familiar with Explorer 3, you may want to select 1 Take a Quick Tour to learn the new features in Explorer 4. Select 2 to learn about Channels.

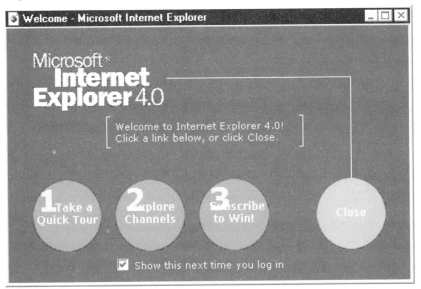

■ To start Internet Explorer, do one of the following:

• Click ![Internet Explorer] on the Desktop.

OR

• Click ![e] on the taskbar.

OR

• Click the Start button ![Start], then select <u>P</u>rograms, Internet Explorer, and click Internet Explorer.

Internet Explorer Screen

■ When you connect to the World Wide Web, the first screen that displays is called a home page. The term home page can be misleading since the first page of *any* World Wide Web site is called a home page. This first page is also sometimes referred to as the start page. You could think of the home/start page as the starting point of your trip on the information highway. Just as you can get on a highway using any number of on ramps, you can get on the Internet at different starting points.

■ You can change the first page that you see when you connect to the Internet. To do this select View, Internet Options, then enter a new address in the Address text box.

√ *The page that you see when you are connected may differ from the one illustrated below.*

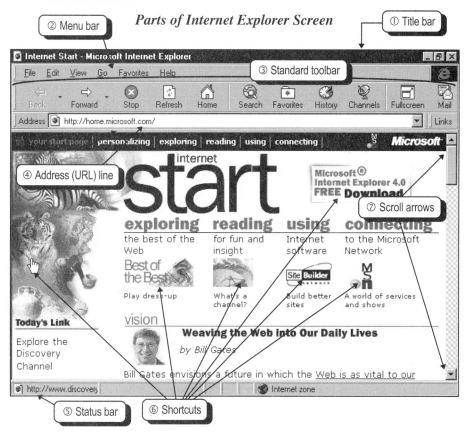

Parts of Internet Explorer Screen

① **Title bar** Displays the name of the program and the current Web page. You can minimize, restore, or close Explorer using the buttons on the right side of the Title bar.

② **Menu bar** Displays menus currently available, which provide drop-down lists of commands for executing Internet Explorer tasks.

  The Internet Explorer icon on the right side of the Menu bar rotates when action is occurring or information is being processed.

③ **Standard toolbar** Displays frequently used commands.

④ **Address (URL) line** Displays the address of the current page. You can click here, type a new address, press Enter, and go to a new location (if it's an active Web site). You can also start a search from this line.

If you click on the arrow at the right end of the address line, you will see the links that you have visited during the current Internet session. The Links bar, containing links to various Microsoft sites is concealed on the right side of the address bar. Drag the split bar to the left or somewhere else on the screen to display current Links. If you double-click the Links button, all the current links will display. Double-click again to hide the links on the right side of the menu bar. You can add/delete links.

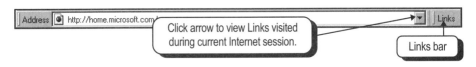

Links button

Buttons on Links bar

Note in the illustration above that the Links button has moved to the left side of the address bar. Just double-click on the Links button again to restore the address line. You can also drag the move bar, next to the Links button, to the left so that the Links and the Address line will both display. Drag the Links button down to display the contents of the Links bar directly below the Address bar (see illustration below).

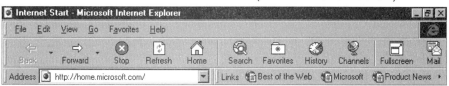

⑤ **Status bar**   Displays information about actions occurring on the page and the Security Level. Internet Security Properties lets you control content that is downloaded on to your computer.

⑥ **Shortcuts**   Click on shortcuts (also called hyperlinks) to move to other Web sites. Shortcuts are usually easy to recognize. They can be underlined text, text of different colors, "buttons" of various sizes and shapes, or graphics. An easy way to tell if you are pointing to a shortcut is by watching the mouse pointer as it moves over the page. When it changes to a hand, you are on a shortcut. When you point to a shortcut the full name of the Web site will appear on the Status bar.

⑦ **Scroll**   Scroll arrows are used to move the screen view, as in
   arrows   all Windows applications.

Exit Internet Explorer

■ Exiting Internet Explorer and disconnecting from your service provider are two separate steps. It is important to remember that if you close Internet Explorer (or any other browser), you must also disconnect (or hang up) from your service provider. If you don't disconnect, you'll continue incurring charges.

CAUTION *When you exit Internet Explorer, you do not necessarily exit from your Internet service provider. Be sure to check the disconnect procedure from your ISP so that you will not continue to be charged for time online. Some services automatically disconnect when a specific amount of time has passed with no activity.*

Microsoft Internet Explorer: 8

◆ **Standard Toolbar Buttons**
◆ **Open a World Wide Web Site from the Address Bar**
◆ **Open a World Wide Web Site Using the File Open Dialog Box**

Internet Explorer Toolbar

Standard Toolbar Buttons

■ The **Internet Explorer Standard toolbar** displays frequently used commands. If the Standard toolbar is *not* visible when you start Explorer, open the View menu, select Toolbars, then select Standard Buttons.

 Moves back through pages previously displayed. Back is available only if you have moved around among Web pages in the current Navigator session; otherwise, it is dimmed.

 Moves forward through pages previously displayed. Forward is available only if you have used the Back button; otherwise, it is dimmed.

 Interrupts the opening of a page that is taking too long to display. Some pages are so filled with graphics, audio, or video clips that delays can be expected.

 Reloads the current page.

 Returns you to your home page. You can change your home page to open to any Web site or a blank page (View, Internet Options, General).

 Allows you to select from a number of search services with a variety of options.

 Displays the Web sites that you have stored using the features available on the Favorites menu. Click Favorites button again to close the Favorites.

Displays links to Web sites that you have visited in previous days and weeks. You can change the number of days that sites are stored in your History folder (View, Internet Options). Click the History button again to close the History window.

 Displays the list of current channels on the Explorer bar. Click again to close the Channels window.

 Conceals Menu, titles, Status bar, and address line to make available the maximum screen space possible for viewing a Web page. Click it again to restore Menu, titles, Status bar, and address line.

 Displays a drop-down menu with various Mail and News options. You will learn about Outlook Express e-mail options in Chapters 10-12.

Open a World Wide Web Site from the Address Bar

■ Click in the Address bar and start typing the address of the Web site you want to open. If you have visited the site before, Internet Explorer will try to complete the address automatically. If it is the correct address, press Enter to go to it. If it is not the correct address, type over the suggested address that displayed on the line. To see other possible matches, click the down arrow. If you find the one you want, click on it.

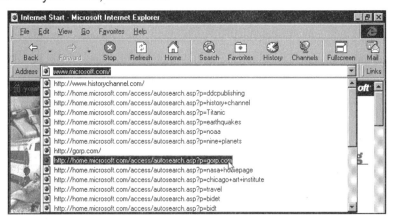

■ To turn off the AutoComplete feature, open the View menu, select Internet Options, and click the Advanced tab. Deselect Use AutoComplete in the Browsing area of the dialog box.

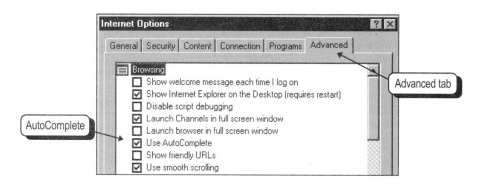

Open a World Wide Web Site Using the File Open Dialog Box

- Select File, Open, and start entering the exact address of the site you want to open. If AutoComplete is turned on and Explorer finds a potential match for the site, it will automatically appear on this line. If the match is the site you want to open, press Enter to go there. If you want to see other possible matches, click the down arrow in the open dialog box.

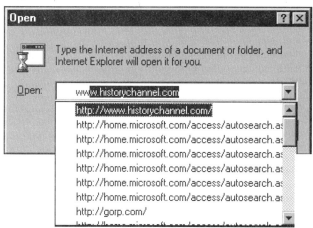

√ *Other ways of opening Web sites will be explored in this lesson. Chapters 19-21 will explain how to search for sites whose exact addresses you do not know.*

◆ **Open and Add to the Favorites Folder**
◆ **Open Web Sites from the Favorites Folder**
◆ **Create New Folders in the Favorites Folder**
◆ **AutoSearch from the Address Bar**

Open and Add to the Favorites Folder

■ As you spend more time exploring Web sites, you will find sites that you want to visit frequently. You can store shortcuts to these sites in the **Favorites folder**.

■ To add a site to the Favorites folder, first go to the desired Web site. Open the F̲avorites menu or right-click anywhere on the page and select Add To F̲avorites.

■ The following dialog box appears when you select Add to F̲avorites.

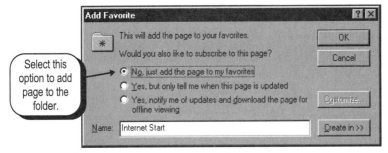

■ The name of the Page you have opened appears in the N̲ame box. There are three ways you can store the address in response to the question "Would you also like to subscribe to this page?" Subscribing to a page means you can schedule automatic updates to that site.

• N̲o, just add the page to my favorites
Puts a shortcut to the Web site in your Favorites folder.

• Y̲es, but only tell me when this page is updated
Explorer will alert you when an update to the site is available.

• Yes, notify me of updates and d̲ownload the page for offline viewing
Explorer will automatically download and update to your computer.

■ Click OK to add the Web address to the Favorites folder.

Open Web Sites from the Favorites Folder

- Click the Favorites button ![Favorites] on the Standard toolbar to open Web sites from the Favorites folder. The Explorer bar will open on the left side of the Browser window.

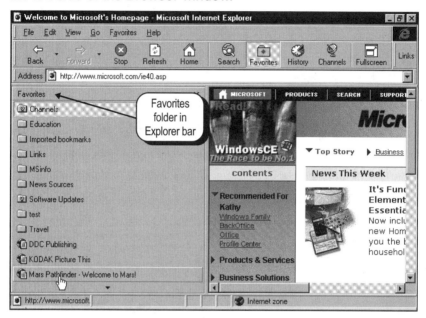

- Click on an address or open a folder and select a site. Close the Explorer bar by clicking the close button or the Favorites button on the toolbar.

- You can also open the Favorites menu and select a site from the list or from a folder.

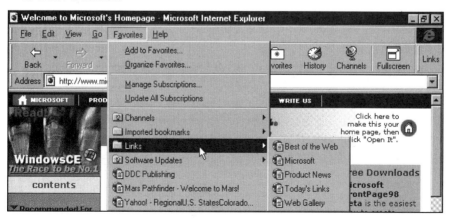

Create New Folders in the Favorites Folder

- You can create new folders before or after you have saved addresses in your Favorites folder.

  - Click Favorites and select Organize Favorites.
  - Click the Create New Folder button (shown in illustration below).

  - Type the name of the new folder and press Enter.

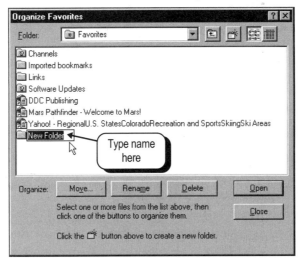

AutoSearch from the Address Bar

- In addition to displaying and entering addresses in the Address bar, you can use AutoSearch to perform a quick search directly from the Address bar.

- Click once in the Address bar and type *go, find,* or *?* and press the spacebar once. Enter the word or phrase you want to find and press Enter. For example, if you want to search for information about the year 2000, type "Find the year 2000" on the Address bar and press Enter.

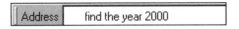

■ Note the Status bar displays the message "Finding site…" It is actually finding a search site. In a few moments, the results of your search displays. The keywords in your search appear in bold in the list of links that are relevant to the search string that you entered.

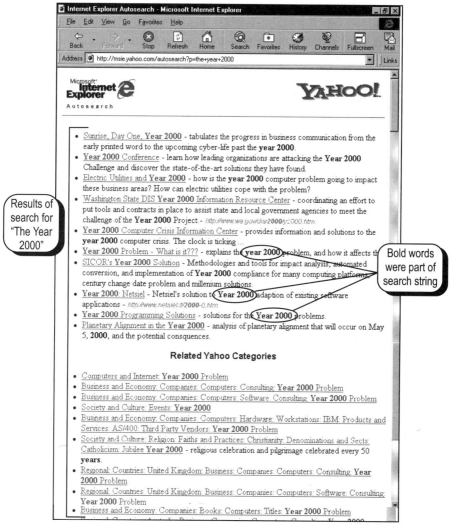

■ AutoSearch uses only one search site. If you want to refine your search or see if other search engines will give you different results, click the Search button [Search] on the Standard toolbar and select a Search provider from the Choose provider drop-down list in the Explorer bar to access a different Search site.

Outlook Express: 10

♦ Configure Outlook Express ♦ Start Outlook Express
♦ Outlook Express Main Window ♦ Retrieve New Messages
♦ The Mail Window ♦ Read Messages ♦ Delete a Message
♦ Print a Message ♦ Save a Message

Configure Outlook Express

√ *This section assumes that you have already set up an e-mail account with a service provider. If you do not have an e-mail address, contact your Internet Service Provider. Establishing a modem connection and configuring your computer to send and receive mail can be frustrating. Don't be discouraged. What follows are steps that will get you connected, but some of the information may have to be supplied by your Internet Service Provider. Calling for help will save you time and frustration.*

■ Outlook Express is the e-mail program included in the Microsoft Internet Explorer 4.0 suite. With this program, you can send, receive, save, and print e-mail messages and attachments.

■ Before you can use Outlook Express to send and receive e-mail, you must configure the program with your e-mail account information (user name, e-mail address, and mail server names).

■ You may have already filled in this information if you completed the Internet Connection Wizard when you started Internet Explorer for the first time. If not, you can enter the information by running the Internet Connection Wizard again.

Internet Connection Wizard

• Launch Outlook Express. Open the Tools menu, select Accounts. Click the Mail tab. Click Add and select Mail to start the Connection Wizard.

• The Internet Connection Wizard will ask for information necessary to set up or add an e-mail account.

• Enter the name you want to appear on the "From" line in your outgoing messages. Click Next.

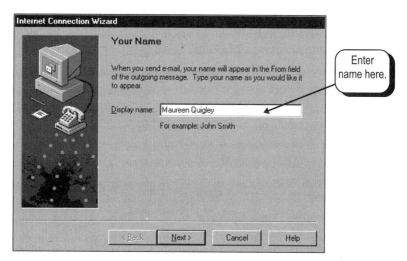

- Type your e-mail address. This is the address that people use to send mail to you. You usually get to create the first part of the address (the portion in front of the @ sign); the rest is assigned by your Internet Service Provider. Click Next.

- Enter the names of your incoming and outgoing mail servers. Check with your Internet Service Provider if you do not know what they are. Click Next.

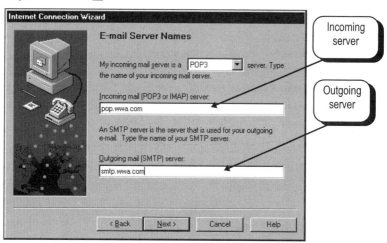

- Enter the logon name that your Internet Service Provider requires for you to access your mail. You will probably also have to enter a password. The password will appear as asterisks (******) to prevent others from knowing it. Click Next when you are finished.

- Enter the name of the account that will appear when you open the Accounts list on the Tools menu in Outlook Express. It can be any name that you choose. Click Next when you have finished.

- Select the type of connection that you are using to reach the Internet. If you are connecting through a phone line, you will need to have a dial-up connection. If you have an existing connection, click Next and select from the list of current connections.

- Select an existing dial-up connection, or select Create a new dial-up connection and follow the directions to create a new one.

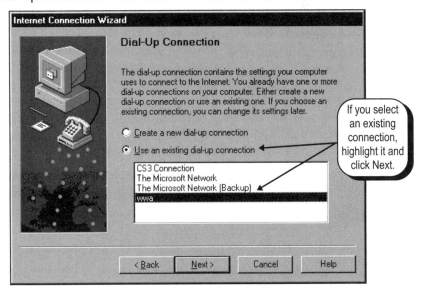

- If you select Use an existing dial-up connection you will click Finish in the last window to save the settings. You should then be able to launch Outlook Express and send and receive mail and attachments.

Start Outlook Express

■ To start Outlook Express:

- Click the Mail icon on the taskbar.

  √ *There is a chance that clicking the Mail icon from the Explorer main window will take you to the Microsoft Outlook organizational program. To use the more compact Outlook Express as your default mail program, click View, Internet Options from the Explorer main window. Click the Programs tab and choose Outlook Express from the Mail pull-down menu.*

  √ *If you downloaded Internet Explorer 4, be sure that you downloaded the standard version, which includes Outlook Express in addition to the Web browser.*

Outlook Express Main Window

■ After you launch Outlook Express, the main Outlook Express window opens by default. You can access any e-mail function from this window.

Outlook Express Main Window

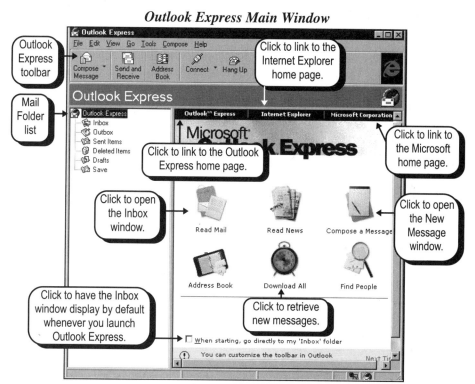

■ Descriptions of items in the main window follow below:

• The **Mail Folder list** displays in the left column of the window, with the Outlook Express main folder selected. To view the contents of a different folder, click on the desired folder in the folder list.

• **Shortcuts** to different e-mail functions are located in the center of the window. Click once on a shortcut to access the indicated task or feature.

• **Hyperlinks** to Microsoft home pages are located at the top of the window. Click once to connect to the indicated home page.

• The **Outlook Express toolbar** displays buttons for commonly used commands. Note that each button contains an image and text that describes the button function. Move your cursor over the button to display specific function information. Clicking any of these buttons will activate the indicated task immediately.

Retrieve New Messages

- You can access the retrieve new mail command from any Outlook Express window. To do so:
  - Click the Send and Receive button 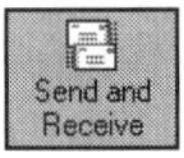 on the toolbar.
- In the Connection dialog box that displays, enter your ISP user name in the User Name text box and your password in the Password text box and click OK. (If you do not know your user name or password, contact your ISP.) Outlook Express will send this information to your ISP's mail server in order to make a connection.

√ *Outlook Express will automatically save your user name and password for the rest of the current Internet session. However, you must re-enter your password each time you reconnect to the Internet or retrieve new mail, unless you set Outlook Express to save your password permanently. To do so, select the* ***Save Password*** *check box in the connection dialog box and click OK.*

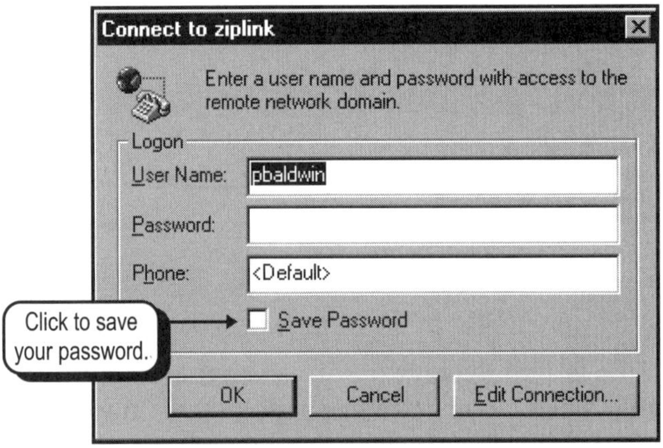

- Once you are connected to the Internet and Outlook Express is connected to your ISP mail server, new mail messages will begin downloading from your ISP mail server. A dialog box displays the status of the transmittal.

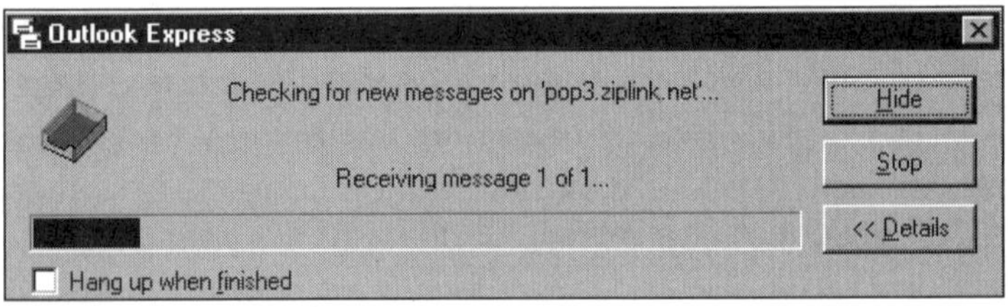

The Mail Window

■ After retrieving new messages, Outlook Express stores them in the Inbox folder.

■ To view your new messages, you must open the Mail window and display the contents of the Inbox folder. To do so:

  • Click the Read Mail shortcut [Read Mail] in the Outlook Express main window.

■ The Mail window opens with the Inbox folder displayed. A description of the items in the Mail window appears on the following page:

Mail Window with Inbox Folder Displayed

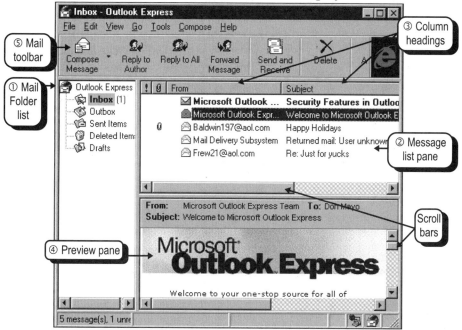

√ *In the message list, unread messages are displayed in bold text with a sealed envelope icon* ✉ *to the left of the header. Messages that have been read are listed in regular text with an open envelope icon* 📭 *to the left of the header.*

① The **Mail Folder list** displays the currently selected message folder, the contents of which are displayed in the mail list. Click on another folder to display its contents in the mail list.

② The **message list pane** displays a header for each of the messages contained in the currently selected mail folder.

③ **Column headings** list the categories of information included in each message header, such as subject, from, and date received. You can customize the display of the header columns in a number of ways:

  - Resize column widths by placing the mouse pointer over the right border of a column heading until the pointer changes to a double arrow and then click and drag the border to the desired size.

  - Rearrange the order of the columns by clicking and dragging a column heading to a new location in the series.

④ The **preview pane** displays the content of the message currently selected from the message list. You can show/hide the preview pane by selecting View, Layout and clicking on the Use preview pane check box. You can resize the preview pane or the message list pane by placing the pointer over the border between the two panes until the pointer changes to a double arrow and then dragging the border up or down to the desired size.

⑤ The **Mail toolbar** displays command buttons for working with messages. These commands vary depending on the message folder currently displayed (Inbox, Sent, Outbox, etc.).

Read Messages

√ *You do not have to be online to read e-mail. You can reduce your online charges if you disconnect from your ISP after retrieving your messages and read them offline.*

■ You must have the Mail window open and the mail folder containing the message to read displayed.

■ You can read a message in the preview pane of the Mail window, or in a separate window.

■ To read a message in the preview pane, click on the desired message header in the message list. If the message does not appear, select View, Layout, Use preview pane.

■ To open and read a message in a separate window, double-click on the desired message header in the message list.

  √ *The Message window opens displaying the Message toolbar and the contents of the selected message.*

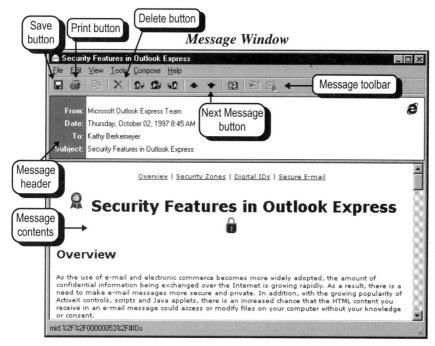

Message Window

- You can close the Message window after reading a message by clicking File, Close or by clicking on the Close button (X) in the upper-right corner of the window.

- Use the scroll bars in the Message window or the preview pane to view hidden parts of a displayed message. Or, press the down arrow key to scroll down through the message.

- To read the next unread message:

  • Select View, Next, Next Unread Message.

  OR

  • If you are viewing a message in the Message window, click the Next button [▼] on the Message toolbar.

- Once you have read a message, it remains stored in the Inbox folder until you delete it or file it in another folder. (See "Delete a Message" on the following page.)

Delete a Message

■ To delete a message:

• Select the desired header from the message list in the Mail window.

• Click the Delete button 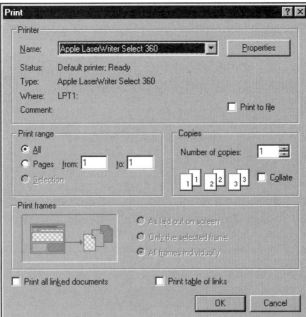 in the Mail toolbar, or select Edit, Delete.

  OR

• Open the desired message in the Message window.

• Click the Delete button ☒ on the Message toolbar.

  √ *To select more than one message to delete, click the Ctrl button while you click each message header.*

Print a Message

■ To print a message:

• Select the message you want to print from the message list in the Mail window or open the message in the Message window.

• Select Print from the File menu.

• In the Print dialog box that opens, select the desired print options and click OK.

Print Dialog Box

■ You can bypass the Print dialog box and send the message to the printer using the most recently used print settings by opening the message in the Message window and clicking the Print button 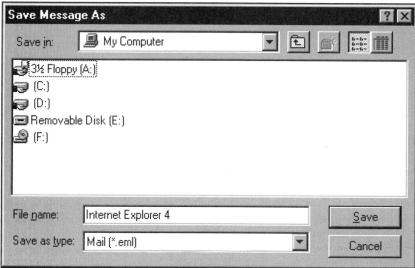 on the Message toolbar.

Save a Message

■ To save a message to your hard drive:

• Open the desired message in the Message window and click the Save button 💾 on the Message toolbar.

• In the Save Message As dialog box that opens, click the Save in drop-down list box and select the drive and folder in which to store the message file.

Save Messages As

• Click in the File name box and enter a name for the message.

• Click Save.

◆ Compose New Messages ◆ Send Messages ◆ Reply to Mail
◆ Forward Mail ◆ Add Entries to the Personal Address Book
◆ Address a New Message Using the Personal Address Book

Compose New Messages

■ You can compose an e-mail message in Outlook Express while you are connected to the Internet, or while you are offline. When composing an e-mail message online, you can send the message immediately after creating it. When composing a message offline, you will need to store the message in your Outbox folder until you are online and can send it. (See "Send Messages" on page 56.)

■ To create a message, you first need to open the New Message window. To do so:

• Click the New Mail Message button [Compose Message] on the toolbar in either the Mail window or the Main window.

The New Message window displays (see the next page).

√ *You can hide any toolbar in the New Message window by going to the View menu and deselecting Toolbar, Formatting Toolbar, or Status Bar.*

• In the New Message window, type the Internet address(es) of the message recipient(s) in the To field.

√ *If you type the first few characters of a name or e-mail address that is saved in your address book, Outlook Express will automatically complete it for you. (See page 60 for information on using the Address Book.)*

OR

Click the Index Card icon [icon] in the To field or the Address Book button [icon] on the New Message toolbar and select an address to insert (see page 60 for information on using the Address Book).

√ *If you are sending the message to multiple recipients, insert a comma or semicolon between each recipient's address.*

54

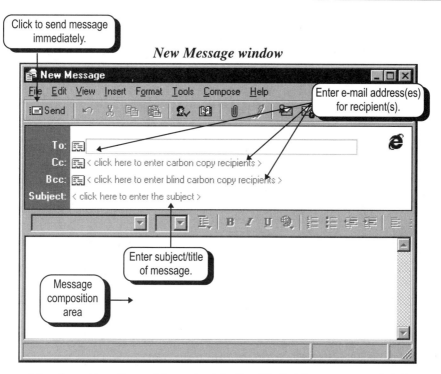

New Message window

- After inserting the address(es) in the To field, you may click in either of the following fields and enter the recipient information indicated.

CC (Carbon Copy)	The e-mail addresses of people who will receive copies of the message.
BCC (Blind Carbon Copy)	Same as CC, except these names will not appear anywhere in the message, so other recipients will not know that the person(s) listed in the BCC field received a copy.

- Click in the Subject field and type the subject of the message. An entry in this field is required.

- Click in the blank composition area below the Subject field and type the body of your message. Wordwrap occurs automatically, and you can cut and paste quotes from other messages or text from other programs. You can also check the spelling of your message by selecting Spelling from the Tools menu and responding to the prompts that follow.

Send Messages

- Once you have created a message, you have three choices:
  - to send the message immediately
  - to store the message in the Outbox folder to be sent later
  - to save the message in the Drafts folder to be edited and sent later

To send a message immediately:

√ *To be able to send messages immediately, you must first select Options from the Tools menu in the Mail window. Then click on the Send tab and select the Send messages immediately check box. If this option is not selected, clicking the Send button will not send a message immediately, but will send the message to your Outbox until you perform the Send and Receive task.*

- Click the send button 〔🖃 Send〕 on the New Message toolbar.

  OR

  Click File, Send Message.

- Outlook Express then connects to your ISP's mail server and sends out the new message. If the connection to the mail server is successful, the sending mail icon displays in the lower-right corner of the status bar until the transmittal is complete:

- Sometimes, however, Outlook Express cannot immediately connect to the mail server and instead has to store the new message in the Outbox for later delivery. When this happens, the sending mail icon does not appear, and the number next to your Outbox folder increases by one 〔 🐦 **Outbox** [1]〕.

- Outlook Express does not automatically reattempt to send a message after a failed connection. Instead, you need to manually send the message from the Outbox (see "To send messages from your Outbox folder" on page 57).

To store a message in your Outbox folder for later delivery:

- Select File, Send Later in the New Message window.

- The Send Mail prompt displays, telling you that the message will be stored in our Outbox folder.

- Click OK.

- The message is saved in the Outbox.

56

To send messages from your Outbox folder:

- Click on the Send and Receive button 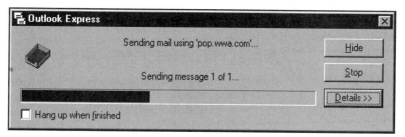 on the toolbar.

  OR

- Click Tools, Send and Receive, All Accounts.

√ *When you use the Send and Receive command, Outlook Express sends out **all** messages stored in the Outbox and automatically downloads any new mail messages from the mail server.*

- After you click Send and Receive, a dialog box opens, displaying the status of the transmittal.

To save a message to your Drafts folder:

- Click File, Save.

- The Saved Message prompt displays. Click OK.

To edit and send message drafts:

- In the Mail window, click in the Drafts folder from the Mail Folder list.

- Double-click on the desired message header from the message list.

- In the New Message window that appears, edit your message as necessary. When you are finished, select File, Send Message to send the message immediately, or File, Send Later to store it in the Outbox folder for later delivery.

■ Outlook Express automatically saves all sent messages in the Sent Items folder. To view a list of the messages you have sent, select the Sent Items folder ▣ Sent Items from the Mail Folder list. The contents will display in the message list pane.

Reply to Mail

■ In Outlook Express, you can reply to a message automatically, without having to enter the recipient's name or e-mail address.

■ When replying, you have a choice of replying to the author and all recipients of the original message or to the author only.

■ To reply to the author and all recipients:

• Select the message you want to reply to from the message list in the Mail window.

• Click the Reply to All button Reply to All on the Mail toolbar.

OR

• Right-click on the selected message and select Reply to All.

■ To reply to the author only:

• Click the Reply to Author button Reply to Author on the Mail toolbar.

OR

• Right-click on the selected message and select Reply to Author.

■ Once you have selected a reply command, the New Message window opens with the address fields and the Subject filled in for you.

√ You can access all of the mail send commands by right-clicking on the message in the Message list.

- The original message is automatically included in the body of your response. To turn off this default insertion, select Options from the Tools menu, click on the Send tab, deselect the Include message in reply check box, and click OK.

- To compose your reply, click in the composition area and type your text as you would in a new message.

- When you are done, click the Send button ⌐≡⌐ Send on the New Message toolbar to send the message immediately. Or, select Send Later from the File menu to store the message in the Outbox folder for later delivery. To save the reply as a draft to be edited and sent later, select Save from the File menu.

Forward Mail

- To forward a message automatically without having to enter the message subject:

  - Select the message to forward from the message list in the Mail window.

  - Click the Forward Message button ⬚ on the Mail toolbar.

    The New Message window opens with the original message displayed and the Subject field filled in for you.

- Fill in the e-mail address information by either typing each address or selecting the recipients from your address book. (See "Address a New Message Using the Personal Address Book" on page 62.)

  √ *If you are forwarding the message to multiple recipients, insert a comma or semicolon between each recipient's address.*

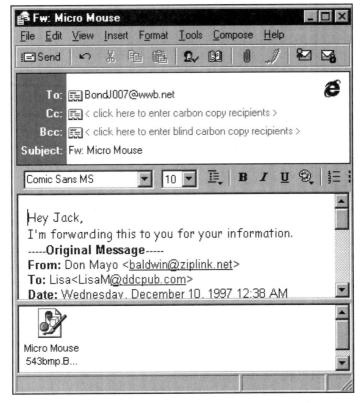

- Click in the composition area and type any text you wish to send with the forwarded message.

- When you are done, click the Send button ⊟Send on the New Message toolbar to send the message immediately. Or, select Send Later from the File menu to store the message in the Outbox folder for later delivery. To save the reply as a draft to be edited and sent later, select Save from the File menu.

Add Entries to the Personal Address Book

- In Outlook Express, you can use the Windows Address Book to store e-mail addresses and other information about your most common e-mail recipients. You can then use the Address Book to find and automatically insert addresses when creating new messages.

- To open the Windows Address Book:

  - Click the Address Book button [Address Book] on the toolbar in the Mail window or the Main window.

60

The Address Book window opens, displaying a list of contacts.

Address Book Window

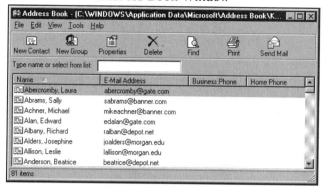

■ To add a name to the address book:

- Click the New Contact button ![New Contact] on the Address Book toolbar.

- In the Properties dialog box that displays, type the First, Middle and Last names of the new contact in the appropriate text boxes.

- Type the contact's e-mail address in the Add new text box and then click the Add button. You can repeat this procedure if you wish to list additional e-mail addresses for the contact.

- In the Nickname text box, you can enter a nickname for the contact (the nickname must be unique among the entries in your address book). When addressing a new message, you can type the nickname in the To field, rather than typing the entire address, and Outlook Express will automatically complete the address.

Contact Properties Dialog Box

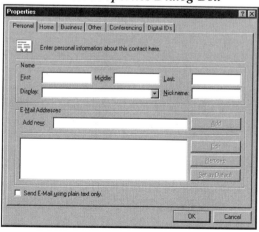

- You can automatically add the name and address of the sender of a message by opening the message in the Message window, right-clicking on the sender's name in the To field, and selecting A<u>d</u>d to Address Book from the shortcut menu.

- You can also set Outlook Express to add the address of recipients automatically when you reply to a message. To do so, select Options from the <u>T</u>ools menu and select the A<u>u</u>tomatically put people I reply to in my Address Book check box on the General tab.

- You can edit an Address Book entry at any time by double-clicking on the person's name in the contact list in the Address Book window.

Address a New Message Using the Personal Address Book

- To insert an address from your address book into a new message:

  - Click the Select Recipients button 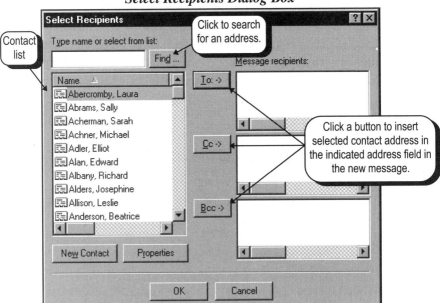 on the New Message toolbar.

  - In the Select Recipients dialog box that follows, select the address to insert from the contact list.

Select Recipients Dialog Box

- Click the button for the field in which you want to insert the address (<u>T</u>o, <u>C</u>c, or <u>B</u>cc). Click OK to return to the New Message window when you are finished.

Outlook Express: 12

♦ **View Attached Files** ♦ **Save Attached Files** ♦ **Attach Files to a Message**

View Attached Files

- Sometimes an e-mail message will come with a separate file(s) attached. Messages containing attachments are indicated in the message list in the Mail window by a paperclip icon 🔋 to the left of the message header.

- If the selected message is displayed in the preview pane, a larger paper clip attachment icon will appear to the right of the header at the top of the preview pane.

Mail Window

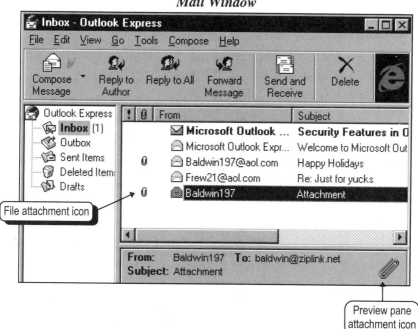

- If you open the selected message in its own window, an attachment icon will appear in a separate pane below the message.

■ To view an attachment:

● Open the folder containing the desired message in the Mail window.

● Select the message containing the desired attachment(s) from the message list to display it in the preview pane.

If the attachment is an image, it will display in the message.

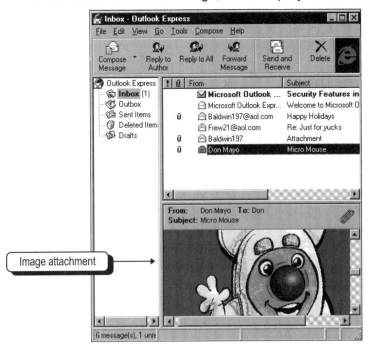

√ *If the image does not display, click Tools, Options, click the Read tab, select the Automatically show picture attachments in messages check box, and click OK.*

■ Other types of attachments, such as a program, word processor document, or media clip, do not display in the message, but have to be opened in a separate window. To do so:

  • Click on the attachment icon 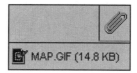 in the preview pane. A button will display with the file name and size of the attachment.

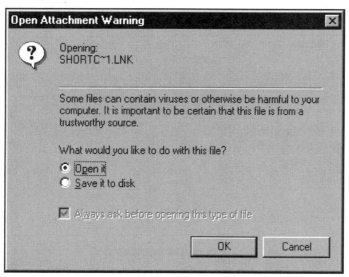

  • Click on this button.
  • If the Open Attachment Warning dialog box displays, select the Open it option and click OK.

■ Outlook Express will open the attached file or play the attached media clip.

■ If the attached file does not open, Outlook Express does not recognize the file type of the attached file (that is, Outlook Express does not contain the plug-in, or your computer does not contain the application needed to view it).

■ To view an unrecognized attachment, you have to install and/or open the application or plug-in needed to view it.

Save Attached Files

■ If desired, you can save an attached file to your hard drive or disk for future use or reference. To save an attachment:

● Select Save Attachments from the File menu, and select the attachment to save from the submenu that displays.

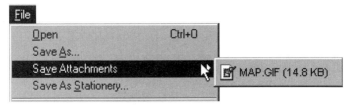

OR

● Right-click on the attachment icon  in the Message window and select the Save As option.

● In the Save As dialog box that follows, click the Save in drop-down list box and select the drive and folder in which to save the file.

Save As Dialog Box

● Click in the File name text box and type a name for the file.
● Click Save.

Attach Files to a Message

■ You can attach a file to an e-mail message while composing the message in the New Message window. To add an attachment:

• Click the Attachments button 📎 on the New Message toolbar.

  OR

• Click Insert, File Attachment.

• In the Insert Attachment dialog box that appears, click the Look in drop-down list box and select the drive and folder containing the file to attach. Then select the file and click Attach.

Insert Attachment Dialog Box

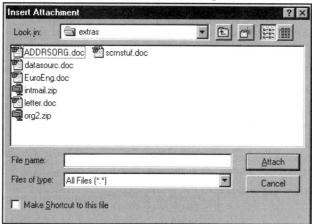

√ *The attachment will appear as an icon in the body of the message.*

√ *Messages containing attachments usually take longer to send than those without attachments.*

√ *When attaching very large files or multiple files, you may want to zip (compress) the files before attaching them. To do so, both you and the recipient need a file compression program, such as WinZip or PKZip.*

New Message Dialog Box

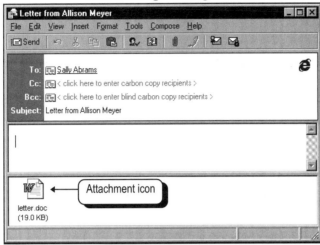

- You can also attach a file by dragging the desired file from your desktop or from Windows Explorer into the New Message window.

- You can add multiple attachments by repeating the procedure as many times as you like.

- Before you send a message containing an attachment, you may wish to make sure the recipient's e-mail program can decode the file you are sending.

◆ **About America Online** ◆ **Start America Online**
◆ **The AOL Home Page, Menu, and Toobar** ◆ **AOL Help** ◆ **Exit AOL**

About America Online?

■ America Online (AOL) is an all-purpose online service. Unlike Netscape Navigator or Microsoft Internet Explorer, AOL is not an Internet browser, yet you can browse the Internet using AOL navigation features.

■ Unlike Internet browsers, AOL does not require a separate Internet Service provider for Internet access, nor does it require a separate mail server connection to access e-mail from the AOL Mail Center. When you install AOL, you configure the program to establish a dial-up connection to the AOL server using your modem. All connections to the Internet and the Mail Center are made via the AOL server.

√ *An Internet service provider is a company that provides Internet access.*

Start America Online

■ To start America Online (Windows 95):

• Click the AOL icon [America Online 3.0 for Wind...] on your desktop. This icon should display on your desktop after you install AOL.

OR

Click the Start button [Start], Programs, America Online, America Online for Windows 95.

• Make sure your screen name is displayed in the Select Screen Name box and type in your password in the Enter Password box.

• Click the Sign On button [SIGN ON] to connect to the AOL server.

The AOL Home Page, Menu, and Toolbar

- After you successfully log on to America Online, you will see a series of screens. The final first screen you see is the AOL home page or start page. The AOL home page contains links to daily AOL featured areas as well as links to constant AOL areas such as *Channels* and *What's New*. You can also access your mailbox from the home page.

Home Screen Menu

- The AOL menu displays options currently available. Click the heading to display a drop-down menu of links to AOL areas and basic filing, editing, and display options.

America Online Toolbar

- The AOL toolbar contains buttons for AOL's most commonly used commands. Choosing a button activates the indicated task immediately.

	You have new mail if the flag on the mailbox is in the up position. Click to display a list of new mail in your mailbox.
	Compose and Send Mail Messages. Displays the Composition screen for composing new mail messages.

70

	Channels are areas of interest arranged by category. AOLs 21 channels offer hundreds of AOL areas and Web site connections.
	New and exciting AOL areas to explore including new AOL features, areas, and special interest sites.
	People Connection takes you to the AOL chat area. Here you can access the AOL Community Center, Chat Rooms, and meet the stars in the Live chat forum.
	File Search opens the search window to the software library where you can download hundreds of software programs.
	Stocks and Portfolios links you to the latest stock market quotes, research a company or mutual fund, or find the latest financial news.
	This area not only brings you the latest headline news, weather, and sports but also allows you to search news archives by keywords. You can also see multimedia (slide show and audio) presentations of the hottest topics in the news.
	Connects you to the Web.
	Shop Online in the AOL Marketplace. Goods and services are categorized for your convenience.
	Lets you customize AOL to suit your needs. Each member area shows you step-by-step how to access and select options.
	Click to see an estimate of how long you have been online for the current session.
	Click to print whatever is displayed on your computer screen. Opens the Print dialog box where you can select from the standard print options.
	The Personal Filing Cabinet is a storage area located on your hard disk used to organize files such as downloaded e-mail messages, files, and newsgroup messages.
	Click this icon to create links or shortcuts to your favorite Web sites or AOL areas.
	This is a quick way to access the AOL member directory and to find answers to questions.
	Displays an area called Find Central. Go here to search the AOL directory using keywords and phrases.
	Each AOL area has a keyword to identify the area. Enter the Keyword for immediate access to the desired AOL area.

AOL Help

■ AOL offers extensive Help so that you can learn to use AOL effectively and find answers to any questions you may have about either AOL or the Web. All AOL topics can be printed or saved to your hard disk.

■ To access Help, click Help and the help topic of choice from the menu.

Exit AOL

■ To exit AOL, click the close window button ⊠ in the upper-right corner of the AOL screen.

OR

Click Sign Off, Sign Off on the menu bar.

OR

Click File, Exit. ·

◆ **Access the Internet from AOL** ◆ **Open a Wold Wide Web Site**
◆ **The AOL Browser Screen** ◆ **Stop a Load or Search**

Access the Internet from AOL

■ To go to the Internet Connection:

- Click the Internet button ⊕ on the AOL main screen.

  OR

- Click **internet** from the Channels menu.

  OR

- Press Ctrl+K, type internet in the Keyword box and press Enter.
  The Internet Connection window displays.

Open a World Wide Web Site

■ If you know the Web address (URL), type it into the Type in Web Address below box and click the GO TO THE WEB button

GO TO THE WEB or press Enter. If the Web address is correct, you will be connected to the Web site.

■ If you wish to search the Internet, click the GO TO AOL NETFIND button **GO TO AOL NETFIND**.

The AOL Browser Screen

■ Once you are connected to the Web, the screen elements change, and the Browser toolbar displays.

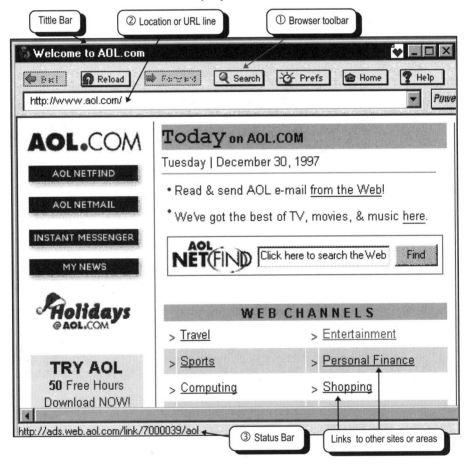

① **Browser Toolbar**

- The AOL Browser toolbar will help you navigate through sites you visit on the Web. Buttons on the Browser toolbar also connect you to search and Internet preference areas.

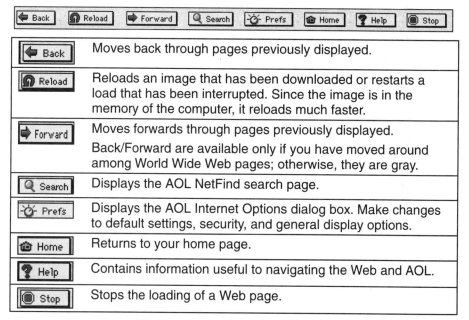

Back	Moves back through pages previously displayed.
Reload	Reloads an image that has been downloaded or restarts a load that has been interrupted. Since the image is in the memory of the computer, it reloads much faster.
Forward	Moves forwards through pages previously displayed. Back/Forward are available only if you have moved around among World Wide Web pages; otherwise, they are gray.
Search	Displays the AOL NetFind search page.
Prefs	Displays the AOL Internet Options dialog box. Make changes to default settings, security, and general display options.
Home	Returns to your home page.
Help	Contains information useful to navigating the Web and AOL.
Stop	Stops the loading of a Web page.

② **Location Line**

- AOL stores each Web address you visit during each AOL session. If you wish to return to an address you have visited during the current session, you can click the location box arrow and click the address from the pull-down list.

③ Status Bar

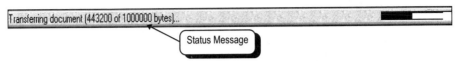

- The Status bar, located at the bottom of the screen, is a helpful indicator of the progress of the loading of a Web page. For example, if you are loading a Web site, you will see the byte size of the page, the percentage of the task completed, and the number of graphics and links yet to load. In many cases the time it will take to load the page will display.

Stop a Load or Search

- Searching for information or loading a Web page can be time-consuming, especially if the Web page has many graphic images, if a large number of people are trying to access the site at the same time, or if your modem and computer operate at slower speeds. If data is taking a long time to load, you may wish to stop a search or the loading of a page or large file.

- To stop a search or load:

  - Click the Stop button ⬤ Stop on the Navigation toolbar.

- If you decide to continue the load after clicking the Stop button, click the Reload button 🔄 Reload.

America Online: 15

◆ **Favorite Places** ◆ **Add Favorite Places** ◆ **View Favorite Places**
◆ **Delete Favorite Places** ◆ **AOL History List**
◆ **Save Web Pages** ◆ **Print Web Pages**

Favorite Places

- A **Favorite Place** listing is a bookmark that you create containing the title, URL, and a direct link to a Web page or AOL area that you may want to revisit. A Favorite Place listings links directly to the desired page.

- The AOL Favorite Place feature allows you to maintain a record of Web sites in your Favorite Places file so that you can return to them easily. (See "Add Favorite Places" below.)

Add Favorite Places

- There are several ways to mark an AOL area or Web site and save it as a Favorite Place. Once the page is displayed:

  - Click the Favorite Place heart 💟 on the Web site or AOL area title bar.

TUCOWS World Wide Affiliate Site Locations! 💟 🔲 🗖 ⊠

  - Click Yes to confirm the addition of the listing.

    Favorite
    Place icon

  OR

  - Display the Web page to add, right-click anywhere on the page and select Add to <u>F</u>avorites from the shortcut menu.

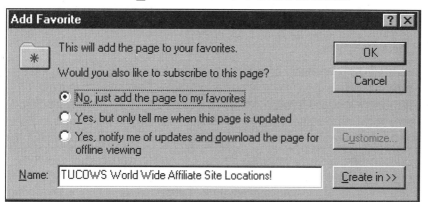

America Online (AOL) 77

- Click the desired option from the confirmation box that displays and click OK.
- The site will automatically be added to your Favorite Places list.

View Favorite Places

■ You can view the Favorite Places file by selecting G̲o To, Favorite Places, or by clicking on the Favorite Places button [image] on the AOL toolbar. Click on any listing from the list to go directly to that page.

■ The details of any Favorite Place listing can be viewed or modified by using the buttons on the Favorite Places screen.

Delete Favorite Places

■ You may wish to delete a Favorite Place if a Web site no longer exists or remove an AOL area from the listing that is no longer of interest to you.

To delete a Favorite Place:

- Click the Favorite Places button [image] on the toolbar.
- Click on the listing to delete.
- Click the Delete button Delete from the Favorite Places screen.
  OR
- Right-click on the listing and select Delete from the pop-up menu.
  OR
- Press the Delete key.
- Click YES to confirm the deletion.

AOL History List

■ While you move back and forth within a Web site, AOL automatically records each page location. The history is only temporary and is deleted when you sign-off. AOL areas are not recorded in the history list.

■ To view the history list, click on the arrow at the end of the URL line. You can use History to jump back or forward to recently viewed pages by clicking on the page from the list.

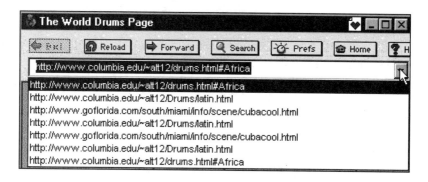

Save Web Pages

- When you find a Web page with information that you would like to keep for future reference, or to review later offline, you can save it to your hard disk. To save a Web page:

  - Click File, Save

  - Type a filename in the File name box.

    √ When you save a Web page, often the current page name appears in the File name box. You can use this name or type a new one.

  - Choose the drive and folder in which to store the file from the Save in drop-down list

  - Click Save.

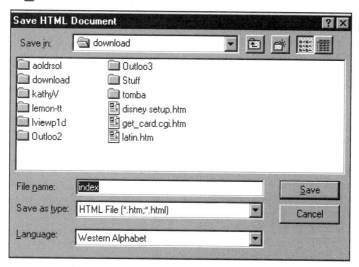

- In most cases when you choose to save a Web page, AOL will automatically save it as an HTML file. Saving a page as an HTML file saves the original formatting and, when accessed, will display as you saw it on the Web.

- You can also save a Web page as a Plain text file which saves only the page text without the formatting or images and placeholders. You might want to do this when saving a very large file, such as a literary work or multiple-page article. To save in Plain text format, click the down arrow next to the Save as type box in the Save As dialog box and select Plain text from the list.

- You can view a saved Web page later by clicking File, Open, and entering the name and location from the Open a File box or by choosing the location and double-clicking on the file name.

Print Web Pages

- One of the many uses of the Internet is to find and print information. You can print a page as it appears on screen, or you can print it as plain text. Only displayed pages can be printed. To print a Web page, display it and do the following:

  - Click the Print button on the AOL toolbar.

    OR

  - Click Print on the File menu.

  - In the Print dialog box that displays, select the desired print options and click OK.

- In most cases, the Web page will be printed in the format shown in the Web page display.

America Online E-mail: 16

◆ **Read New Mail** ◆ **Compose a New Mail Message**
◆ **Send Messages** ◆ **Reply to Mail**
◆ **Forward Mail** ◆ **AOL Mail Help**

Read New Mail

■ There are several ways to know whether you have new mail in your mailbox: If your computer has a sound card and speakers, you will hear "You've Got Mail" when you successfully connect to AOL. The

 link is replaced by the You Have Mail link, and the mailbox

icon on the main screen has the flag in the up position .

To display and read new and unread mail:

• Click the You Have Mail button on the AOL main screen.
  OR

• Click the Read New Mail button [icon] on the main screen toolbar
  OR

• Press Ctrl+R.

  √ *The New Mail list displays new and unread mail for the screen name used for this session. If you have more than one screen name, you must sign on under each name to retrieve new mail.*

  √ *New and Unread e-mail messages remain on the AOL mail server for approximately 27 days before being deleted by AOL. If you want to save a message to your hard disk, click **File, Save As** and choose a location for the message. By default the message will be saved to the Download folder.*

• To read a message, double-click on it from the New Mail list.

Compose a New Mail Message

• Click Mail, Compose Mail.
  OR

• Click the Compose Mail button [icon] on the main screen toolbar.
  OR

• Click Ctrl+M.

The Compose Mail screen displays.

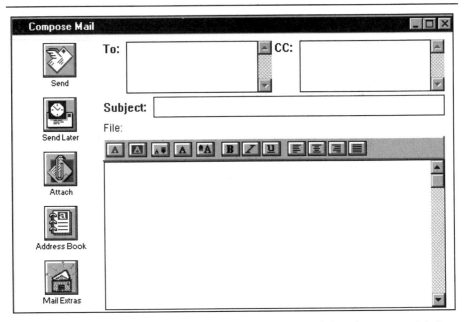

- Fill in the e-mail address(es) in the To box of the Compose Mail screen.

  OR

- Select Address Book and double-click to select an address. (See "America Online E-mail: 18" on page 88 for more information on your Address book.)

- If you are sending the same message to multiple recipients, fill in the CC: (Carbon Copy) box with the e-mail addresses of recipients who will receive a copy of this message. These names will display to all recipients of the message.

- If you want to send BCC: (Blind courtesy copies—copies of a message sent to others but whose names are not visible to the main or other recipients), put the address in parenthesis, for example: (ddcpub.com).

  √ *Multiple addresses must be separated with a comma.*

- Fill in the Subject box with a one-line summary of your message. AOL will not deliver a message without a subject heading. This is the first thing the recipient sees in the list of new mail when your message is delivered.

- Fill in the body of the message.

Send Messages

- Click the Send button to send the message immediately. *You must be online.*

   OR

- Click the Send Later button to send a message later that you have composed offline.

Reply to Mail

- You can reply to mail messages while online or compose replies to e-mail offline to send later.

- To reply to e-mail:

- Click the Reply button from the displayed message screen. If the message has been sent to more than one person, you can send your response to each recipient of the message by

   clicking the Reply to All button. The addresses of the sender and, if desired, all recipients will be automatically inserted into the address fields.

   √   *To include part or all of the original message in your Reply, select the contents of the original message to be included in quotes in your message and click the Reply button to begin your reply.*

- Click the Send button if you are online and want to send

   the reply immediately or click the Send Later button.

Forward Mail

■ There are times when you may want to send mail sent to you on to someone else.

■ To forward e-mail:

• Click the Forward button [Forward] from the displayed message screen and fill in the address(es) of the recipients of the forwarded message. The Subject heading from the original message is automatically inserted into the subject heading box.

• Click the Send button [Send] if you are online and want to send the reply immediately or click the Send Later button [Send Later].

AOL Mail Help

■ For answers to many of your basic e-mail questions, click Mail, Mail Center, and click on the Let's Get Started button [LET'S GET STARTED].

◆ **Add Attachments to a Message**
◆ **Download File Attachments**

Add Attachments to a Message

■ You can attach a file to send along with any e-mail message. Before you send a file attachment—especially if it is a multimedia file—it is a good idea to make sure that the recipient's e-mail program can read the attachment. For example, files sent in MIME format cannot be viewed by AOL e-mail and require separate software to be opened.

To attach files to a message:

• Compose the message to be sent. (See "Compose a New Mail Message" on page 81.)

• Click the Attach button [Attach] on the Compose Message screen.

• Select the drive and folder where the file you wish to attach is located.

• Double-click the file to attach from the Attach File dialog box.
  √ *The attachment will appear below the Subject box.*

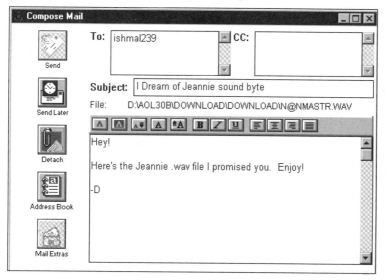

- If you are online, click the Send button [Send] to send the

  message immediately, or click the Send Later button [Send Later] to store the message in your Outgoing Mail if you are working offline.

  √ *Multiple files must be grouped together in a single archive using a file compression program such as PKZIP or WINZIP. Both you and the recipient will need a file compression program.*

Download E-mail File Attachments

■ An e-mail message that arrives with a file attachment is displayed in your new mail list with a small diskette under the message icon.

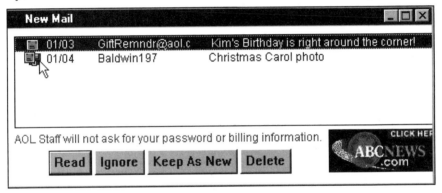

■ Opening the message and viewing the attachment are two separate steps:

- Open the message by double-clicking on it from the New Mail list (see "To display and read new and unread mail" on page 81). The message will display.

- You can choose to download the file attachment immediately by clicking the Download File button [Download File] at the bottom of

  the displayed message screen. Click the Save button [Save] on the Download Manager screen to save the file, by default, to the AOL30/Download folder. If you desire, you can change the save destination folder.

- A status box will display while the attachment is being downloaded or transferred to your computer.

- At the end of the download, the file transfer box will close and you will see the message "File's Done."

OR

- You may choose to download the file later. Click the Download Later button **Download Later** to store the message in the Download Manager. When you are ready to download the file, click File, Download Manager, and then select the file to download. You must be online.

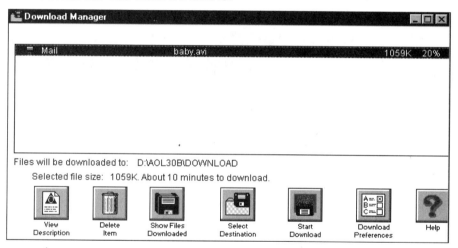

√   *Click Sign off after transfer if you want AOL to automatically disconnect when the transfer is complete.*

To change the default location of where files are stored:

- Click the Select Destination button ![Select Destination] from the Download Manager screen and choose the desired destination from the Select Path dialog box.

◆ **Add Entries to the Address Book**
◆ **Enter an Address Using the Address Book**

Add Entries to the Address Book

■ Once you start sending e-mail, you may be surprised at how many people you start to communicate with online. An easy way to keep track of e-mail addresses is to enter them into the Address Book. Once an e-mail address entry has been created, you can automatically insert it from the Address Book into the address fields.

To create Address Book entries:

• Click <u>M</u>ail, Edit <u>A</u>ddress Book. The Address Book dialog box displays.

• Click the Create button **Create** to open the Address Group box.

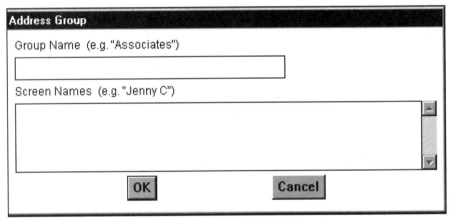

• Enter the real name or nickname of the e-mail recipient (e.g., JohnV) or the name of a Group listing (e.g., Book Club) in the Group Name box. The name you enter in this box is the name that will appear in the Address Book list.

• Press the Tab key to move to the Screen Names box and enter the complete e-mail address of the recipient or the e-mail addresses of everyone in the group listing. When entering multiple addresses such as in a group listing, each address must be separated by a comma (e.g., Baldwin168, BubbaB@ziplink.net, etc.).

- Click OK.
  - √ *When sending mail to AOL members through AOL, you do not need to enter the @aol.com domain information. Enter only their screen name as the e-mail address. For all other Address Book entries you must enter the entire address.*

Delete an Address Book Entry

- Click Mail, Edit Address Book to open the Address Book.
- Click the name to delete.
- Click the Delete button **Delete**.
- Click Yes.
- Click OK to close the Address Book.

Enter an Address Using the Address Book

- Place the cursor in the desired address field.

- Click the Address Book button to open the Address Book.
- Double-click the name or names from the Address Book list to insert in the TO: or CC: address box and click OK.

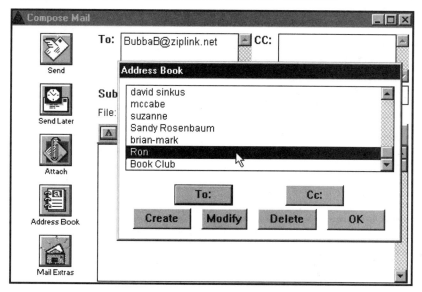

◆ Searching vs. Surfing ◆ Search Sites ◆ Search Basics

Searching vs. Surfing

■ The Web is a vast source of information, but to find information that you want, you must be able to locate it. The Web has many thousands of locations, containing hundreds of thousands of pages of information.

■ Unlike libraries that use either the Library of Congress or Dewey Decimal system to catalog information, the Internet has no uniform way of tracking and indexing information. You can find lots of information on the Internet; the trick is to find information that you want. Initially, it may seem easy to find information on the Web— you just connect to a relevant site and then start clicking on links to related sites. Illustrated below is an example of a search that starts out on one topic and ends on an unrelated one.

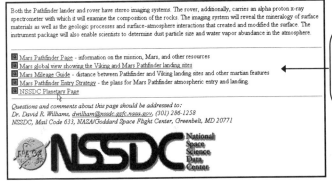

Both the Pathfinder lander and rover have stereo imaging systems. The rover, additionally, carries an alpha proton x-ray spectrometer with which it will examine the composition of the rocks. The imaging system will reveal the mineralogy of surface materials as well as the geologic processes and surface-atmosphere interactions that created and modified the surface. The instrument package will also enable scientists to determine dust particle size and water vapor abundance in the atmosphere.

- Mars Pathfinder Page - information on the mission, Mars, and other resources
- Mars global view showing the Viking and Mars Pathfinder landing sites
- Mars Mileage Guide - distance between Pathfinder and Viking landing sites and other martian features
- Mars Pathfinder Entry Strategy - the plans for Mars Pathfinder atmospheric entry and landing
- NSSDC Planetary Page

Questions and comments about this page should be addressed to:
Dr. David R. Williams, dwilliam@nssdc.gsfc.nasa.gov, (301) 286-1258
NSSDC, Mail Code 633, NASA/Goddard Space Flight Center, Greenbelt, MD 20771

NSSDC National Space Science Data Center

> This Web site contains links to sites about the Mars Pathfinder mission. Click on the link to the National Space Science Data Center.

What's New in Planetary Science

Results of the Mars Pathfinder mission, including a mission summary and APXS Mars surface composition results have been published in *Science* magazine.

- The Mars Global Surveyor resumed its aerobraking activities on November 7th following an analysis of the condition of the solar panels by the project. More detail is available in the NASA press release from the press conference held on 10 November.

- The first 14 volumes of the Clementine Lunar Digital Image Model CD-ROMs are now available from NSSDC. These volumes are regional mosaics created from Clementine images showing the Moon at a resolution of 100 meters/pixel. Volume 15 has lower resolution global views and is expected at the end of 1997.

- Upcoming Planetary Events and Missions
- New and Incoming Planetary Data at NSSDC
- New and Updated Planetary Pages

> This Web site contains links to sites that have broader information about space exploration. Click on the link to Upcoming Planetary Events and Missions.

Upcoming Planetary Events and Missions

Upcoming Planetary Launches and Events

1997 December 16 - <u>Galileo</u> - Europa closest flyby

1998 January 6 - <u>Lunar Prospector</u> - Launch of NASA Global Orbiter Mission to the Moon
1998 January 23 - <u>NEAR</u> - Earth Flyby
1998 April 26 - <u>Cassini</u> - Venus-1 Flyby
1998 July - <u>New Millenium Deep Space-1</u> - Launch of NASA Flyby Mission to Asteroid 3352 McAuliffe and Comet
P/West-Kohoutek-Ikemura
1998 August 6 - <u>Planet-B</u> - Launch of ISAS (Japan) Orbiter Mission to Mars
1998 December - <u>Mars Surveyor '98 Orbiter</u> - Launch of NASA Orbiter Mission to Mars

> Click on Cassini link to go to a Web site that deals with a project to explore Saturn.

Cassini

Cassini has launched!

Launch Date/Time: 15 October 1997 at 08:43 UTC
Launch Vehicle: Titan IV-Centaur
Planned on-orbit mass: 2175 Kg
Power System: Radioisotope Thermal Generators (RTGs) of 630 W

The Cassini Orbiter's mission consists of delivering a probe (called <u>Huygens</u>, provided by ESA) to Titan, and then remaining in orbit around Saturn for detailed studies of the planet and its rings and satellites. The principal objectives are to: (1) determine the three-dimensional structure and dynamical behavior of the rings; (2) determine the composition of the satellite surfaces and

- This is the stream of consciousness method of searching the Internet (**surfing**). It may be interesting and fun to locate information this way, but there are drawbacks. Surfing randomly for information is time consuming and the results are frequently inconsistent and incomplete. It can also be expensive if you are charged fees for connect time to your Internet Service Provider.

- If you want a more systematic and organized way of looking for information, you can connect to one of several search sites that use **search engines** to track, catalog, and index information on the Internet.

Search Sites

- A **search site** builds its catalog using a search engine. A search engine is a software program that goes out on the Web, seeking Web sites, and cataloging them, usually by downloading their home pages.

- Search sites are classified by the way they gather Web site information. All search sites use a search engine in one way or another to gather information. Below is an explanation of how the major search services assemble and index information.

Search Engines

- A search site builds its catalog using a **search engine**. A search engine is a software program that goes out on the Web, seeking Web sites, and cataloging them, usually by downloading their home pages.

- Search engines are sometimes called **spiders** or **crawlers** because they crawl the Web.

- Search engines constantly visit sites on the Web to create catalogs of Web pages and keep them up to date.

- Major search engines include: **AltaVista**, **HotBot**, **Open Text**.

Directories

- Search **directories** catalog information by building hierarchical indexes. Since humans assemble the catalogs, information is often more relevant than the indexes that are assembled by Web crawlers. Directories may be better organized than search engine sites, but they will not be as complete or up-to-date as search engines that constantly check for new material on the Internet.

- **Yahoo**, the oldest search service on the World Wide Web, is the best example of Internet search directories. Other major search directories are: **Infoseek**, **Magellan**, **Lycos**.

Multi-Threaded Search Engines

- Another type of search engine, called a **multi-threaded** search engine, searches other Web search sites and gathers the results of these searches for your use.

- Because they search the catalogs of other search sites, multi-threaded search sites do not maintain their own catalogs. These search sites provide more search options than subject-and-keyword search sites, and they typically return more specific information with further precision. However, multi-threaded search sites are much slower to return search results than subject-and-keyword search sites.

- Multi-threaded search sites include **SavvySearch** and **Internet Sleuth**.

■ If you are using Internet Explorer or Netscape Navigator, you can click on the Search button on the toolbar to access a number of search services.

Search Basics

- When you connect to a search site, the home page has a text box for typing the words you want to use in your search. These words are called a **text string**. The text string may be a single word or phrase, or it may be a complex string which uses **operators** to modify the search (see "Search Engines: 21" for more information on operators). Illustrated below is the opening page of Yahoo, one of the oldest and most popular search directories.

Click to initiate search.

Yahoo! Mail free email

Shop and Win @ NetBuyer

Win a Sports Dream Trip

Search options

Links to Yahoo categories

Yellow Pages - People Search - Maps - Classifieds - Personals - Chat - **Email**
Holiday Shopping - My Yahoo! - News - Sports - Weather - Stoc

Access options to refine search.

- **Arts and Humanities**
  Architecture, Photography, Literature...

- **Business and Economy** [Xtra!]
  Companies, Finance, Employment...

- **Computers and Internet** [Xtra!]
  Internet, WWW, Software, Multimedia...

- **Education**
  Universities, K-12, College Entrance...

- **Entertainment** [Xtra!]
  Cool Links, Movies, Music, Humor...

- **Government**
  Military, Politics [**Xtra!**], Law, Taxes...

- **Health** [Xtra!]
  Medicine, Drugs, Diseases, Fitness...

- **News and Media** [
  Current Events, Magazines, TV, Newspapers...

- **Recreation and Sports** [Xtra!]
  Sports, Games, Travel Autos, Outdoors...

- **Reference**
  Libraries, Dictionaries, Phone Numbers...

- **Regional**
  Countries, Regions, U.S. States...

- **Science**
  CS, Biology, Astronomy, Engineering...

- **Social Science**
  Anthropology, Sociology, Economics...

- **Society and Culture**
  People, Environment, Religion...

Yahooligans! for Kids - Beatrice's Guide - MTV/Yahoo! unfURLed - Yahoo! Internet Life
What's New - Weekly Picks - Today's Web Events
Visa Shopping Guide - Yahoo! Store

Regional links

World Yahoos Australia & NZ - Canada - Denmark - France - Germany - Japan - Korea
Norway - SE Asia - Sweden - UK & Ireland
Yahoo! Metros Atlanta - Austin - Boston - Chicago - Dallas / Fort Worth - Los Angeles
Get Local Miami - Minneapolis / St. Paul - New York - S.F. Bay - Seattle - Wash D.C.

Smart Shopping with **VISA**

How to Suggest a Site - Company Info - Openings at Yahoo! - Contributors - Yahoo! to Go

- Once you have entered a text string, initiate the search by either pressing the Enter key or by clicking on the search button. This button may be called Search, Go Get It, Seek Now, Find, or something similar.
- For the best search results:
  - Always check for misspelled words and typing errors.
  - Use descriptive words and phrases.
  - Use synonyms and variations of words.
  - Find and follow the instructions that the search site suggests for constructing a good search.
  - Eliminate unnecessary words (the, a, an, etc.) from the search string. Concentrate on key words and phrases.
  - Test your search string on several different search sites. Search results from different sites can vary greatly.
  - Explore some of the sites that appear on your initial search and locate terms that would help you refine your search string.

Simple Searches

- Searches can be simple or complex, depending on how you design the search string in the text box.

- A **simple search** uses a text string, usually one or two key words, to search for matches in a search engine's catalog. A simple search is the broadest kind of search.

  - The key words may be specific, such as Internet Explorer browser, current stock quotes, or Macintosh computers, or they may be general, such as software, economy, or computer.

  - The catalog search will return a list, typically quite large, of Web pages and URLs whose descriptions contain the text string you want to find. Frequently these searches will yield results with completely unrelated items.

- When you start a search, the Web site searches its catalog for occurrences of your text string. (Some search sites don't have their own catalog, so they search the catalogs of other search sites.) The results of the search, typically a list of Web sites whose descriptions have words that match your text string are displayed in the window of your browser.

- Each search site has its own criteria for rating the matches of a catalog search and setting the order in which they are displayed.

- The catalog usually searches for matches of the text string in the URLs of Web sites. It also searches for key words, phrases, and meta-tags (key words that are part of the Web page, but are not displayed in a browser) in the cataloged Web pages.

- The information displayed on the results page will vary, depending on the search and display options selected and the search site you are using. The most likely matches for your text string appear first in the results list, followed by other likely matches on successive pages.

  √ *There may be thousands of matches that contain the search string you specified. The matches are displayed a page at a time. You can view the next page by clicking on the "next page" link provided at the bottom of each search results page.*

- For example, if you do a search on the word *Greek*, you'll get results, as illustrated below, that display links to a wide range of links that have something to do with Greek. Note the number of documents that contain the search word.

   √ *These examples use AltaVista to perform the search. Your results may vary with other search tools.*

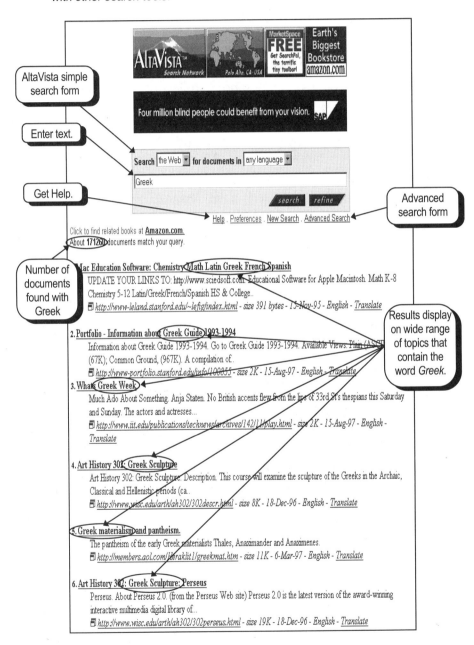

- You can scan the displayed results to see if a site contains the information you are looking for. Site names are clickable links. After visiting a site, you can return to the search site by clicking the Back button on your browser. You can then choose a different site to visit or perform another search.

Refine a Search

- Suppose that you only want to view links that deal with Greek *tragedies*. The natural inclination would be to enter Greek tragedies in the search string to reduce the number of documents that the search tool finds. Note, however, the number of documents that were found when Greek tragedies was entered in this search. Since the search string didn't include a special operator to tell the search engine to look for sites that contain both Greek *and* tragedies, the results display sites that contain Greek *OR* tragedies in addition to sites that contain Greek *AND* tragedies.

- To reduce the number of documents in this search, enter *Greek* press space once, then enter a plus sign (+) and the word tragedies (Greek +tragedies) then click Search. This tells AltaVista to look for articles that contain Greek ***and*** tragedies in the documents. Note the results that display when the plus is added to the search.

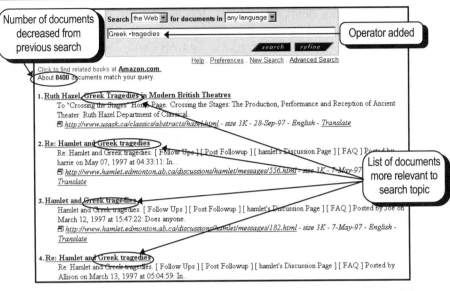

- The number of documents listed is dramatically reduced, and the documents displayed display information that is more closely related to the topic, Greek tragedies.

- You can also *exclude* words by using the minus sign (-) to further refine a search and eliminate unwanted documents in the results. For example, if you wanted to find articles about Greek tragedies but not ones that deal with Hamlet, enter a search string like this: *Greek +tragedies -Hamlet*. Note the different results that display:

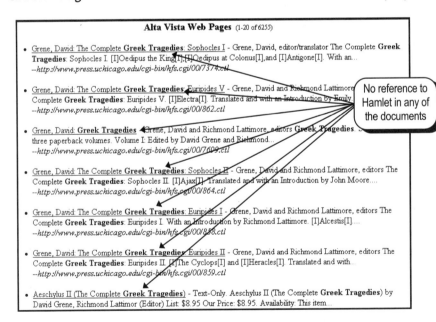

Get Help

■ Check the Help features on the search tool that you are using to see what operators are available. Since there are no standards governing the use of operators, search sites can develop their own. Illustrated on the page 99 are samples of the help available for performing a simple search in AltaVista and Yahoo.

AltaVista Help for Simple Searches

HELP Simple Search

Natural Language queries: (always try this first)

Type a word or phrase or a question (for example, **weather Boston** or **what is the weather in Boston?**), then click Search (or press the Enter key). If the information you want from this sort of query isn't on the first couple of pages, try adding a few more specific words.

Requiring/Excluding Words:

Often you will know a word that will be guaranteed to appear in a document for which you are searching. If this is the case, require that the word appear in all of the results by attaching a "+" to the beginning of the word (for example, to find an article on pet care, you might try the query **dog cat pet +care**). You may also find that when you search on a vague topic, you get a very broad set of results. You can quickly reject results by adding a term that appears often in unwanted articles with a "-" before it (for example, to find a recipe for oatmeal raisin cookies without nuts try **oatmeal raisin cookie -nut* -walnut***).

Exact Phrases:

If you know that a certain phrase will appear on the page you are looking for, put the phrase in quotes. (for example, try entering song lyrics such as **"you ain't nothing but a hound dog"**)

Yahoo Help for Simple Searches

Tips for Better Searching

- **Use Double Quotes Around Words that are Part of a Phrase**

  example |"great barrier reef"| Search

- **Specify Words that Must Appear in the Results**
  Attach a + in front words that *must* appear in result documents.

  example: |sting +police| Search

- **Specify Words that Should Not Appear in the Results**
  Attach a − in front of words that *must not* appear in result documents.

  example: |python -monty| Search

Search Engines: 21

◆ Complex Searches ◆ Operators ◆ Boolean Operators
◆ Plus (+)/Minus (-) System ◆ Grouping Operators
◆ Case Sensitive ◆ Special Characters and Punctuation
◆ Major Search Engines and Operators

Complex Searches

■ When you first connect to a search site, the temptation to type in text and hit the search button is great. Resist it. Taking time to read and understand the search rules of the site will save the time you'll waste by creating a search that yields an overwhelming number of hits. Some of what you want may be buried somewhere in that enormous list, but working your way through the irrelevant sites can waste time, cause frustration, and be very discouraging.

■ In "Search Engines: 20," you learned how simply using a plus or minus sign can create a search that gives a more pertinent list of sites. Now, you will see how to use operators to restrict and refine your searches even more.

Operators

■ A **complex search** usually contains several words in the text string including **operators** that modify the text string. Operators are words or symbols that modify the search string instead of being part of it.

■ Using operators and several descriptive words can narrow your search for information, which means the results will reduce the number of sites that display. This means the resulting list of sites should be more relevant to what you want, thereby saving you time and probably money.

■ Each search site develops its own set of restrictions and options to create searches designed to locate specific information. What follows are some of the commonly used operators and how they are used.

Boolean Operators

- **Boolean operators** specify required words, excluded words, and complex combinations of words to be found during a search. Depending on the site, Boolean operators may be represented by words or symbols.

- The most common Boolean operators are:

AND	The documents found in the search must contain *all words* joined by the AND operator. For example, a search for *Microsoft* AND *Internet* AND *Explorer* will find sites which contain all three words (*Microsoft*, *Internet*, and *Explorer*).
OR	The documents found in the search must contain *at least one of the words* joined by the OR operator. The documents may contain both, but this is not required. For example, a search for *Web* OR *Internet* will find sites which contain either the word *Web* or the word *Internet*.
NOT	The documents found in the search must not contain the word following the NOT operator. For example, a search for *Washington* NOT *DC* will find sites which contain the word *Washington* but none about *Washington DC*.
NEAR	The documents found in the search must contain the words joined by the NEAR operator within a specified number of words, typically ten. For example, *RAM* NEAR memory will find sites with the word *RAM* and the word *memory* within ten words of each other.

- Suppose that you can't remember the name of the earthquake that occurred during the World Series in San Francisco in 1989. If you enter relevant words in the simple search function (using the plus sign) in AltaVista, here's what you get:

> Click to find related books at **Amazon.com**.
> About **18368** documents match your query.
>
> 1. **San Francisco Earthquakes**
> San Francisco Earthquake Links. The Ring of Fire/On Shakey Ground - An Earthquake overview. 1906 Earthquake - Before and After Films. 1906 Earthquake...
> *http://www.exploratorium.edu/earthquake/sf.earthquakes.html* - size 2K - 11-Oct-95 - English
>
> 2. **Why Earthquakes are Inevitable in the San Francisco Bay Area**
> Latest quake info. Hazards & Preparedness. More about earthquakes. Studying Earthquakes. Whats new. Home. Why Earthquakes are Inevitable in the San...
> *http://quake.wr.usgs.gov/hazprep/BayAreaInsert/inevitable.html* - size 3K - 21-Mar-97 - English
>
> 3. **Museums Reach Out With Web Catalogs of Collections /WW November 4 1996**
> Museums Reach Out With Web Catalogs of Collections. By Susan Moran. Earthquakes chase or keep many people away from California. The violent quake of 1989..
> *http://www.webweek.com/96Nov04/markcomm/arts_sake.html* - size 9K - 17-Apr-97 - English
>
> 4. **$A History of California Earthquakes (1 of 101)**
> Content Next. A History of California Earthquakes (Image 1 of 101) Earthquakes in the San Francisco Bay Region. Hayward, 1868. Vacaville, 1892. San...

Results do not answer the question.

- The results display several links to articles about earthquakes in the San Francisco area. If you click on one of these, you may find the earthquake you are looking for.

- Now examine the results of a more complex search using the same words, but using some of the advanced search options available in AltaVista. Entering the search string in the advanced search form of AltaVista displays the following:

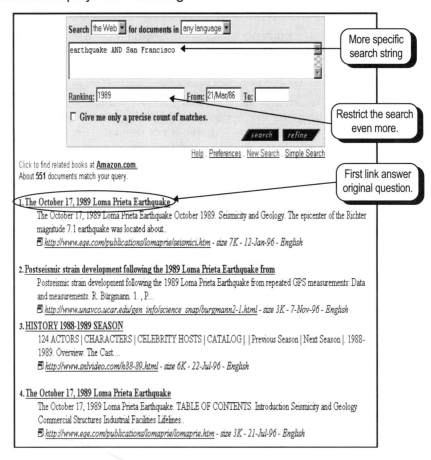

- Use the Advanced search function when you have a specific complex search string; otherwise, use the simple search function. AltaVista will automatically rank the order of the search results when you use the simple search function. When you use the advanced search function, you control the ranking of the results by entering additional search criteria in the Ranking box on the Advanced search form.

Plus (+)/Minus (-) System

■ Boolean logic is the basis for the plus and minus system of constructing a search. If the plus/minus sign is not included in the search string, the search engine assumes that you are using OR. That's why when you searched for *Greek tragedies*, AltaVista looked for documents containing either *Greek* or *tragedies*.

Plus sign (+)   Placed immediately in front of a word (no space between the plus sign and the word) means that all documents found must contain that word. (This is similar to the Boolean AND function.) For example, note the results of a search for articles about earthquakes in California, using a search string like this: *earthquakes +California*.

Click to find related books at **Amazon.com**
About **59247** documents match your query.

1. $A History of California Earthquakes (5 of 101)
   Content Previous Next. A History of California Earthquakes (Image 5 of 101) Earthquake damage in San Francisco Bay Region.
   http://www.johnmartin.com/eqshow/cah_0105.htm - size 399 bytes - 5-Dec-96 - English

2. $A History of California Earthquakes (2 of 101)
   Content Previous Next. A History of California Earthquakes (Image 2 of 101) State map with major fault systems.
   http://www.johnmartin.com/eqshow/cah_0102.htm - size 389 bytes - 5-Dec-96 - English

3. Earthquakes in California
   EARTHQUAKES IN CALIFORNIA. California is the highest earthquake risk area in the contiguous United States. Several large, well-known active faults run...
   http://www.eqe.com/publications/homeprep/eqkesca.htm - size 4K - 26-Nov-95 - English

4. $A History of California Earthquakes (16 of 101)
   Content Previous Next. A History of California Earthquakes (Image 16 of 101) Earthquake damage during the 1957 Daly City earthquake.
   http://www.johnmartin.com/eqshow/cah_0116.htm - size 411 bytes - 5-Dec-96 - English

5. $A History of California Earthquakes (9 of 101)
   Content Previous Next. A History of California Earthquakes (Image 9 of 101) Earthquake damage during the 1868 Hayward earthquake.
   http://www.johnmartin.com/eqshow/cah_0109.htm - size 407 bytes - 5-Dec-96 - English

---

Minus sign (-)   Place immediately in front of a word (again, no space) means that all documents found will NOT contain that word. (This is the Boolean NOT function.) For example, note the results of search for articles about earthquakes that do *not include* California using a search string like this: *earthquakes -California*.

Click to find related books at **Amazon.com**
12985 documents match your query.

1. **IGS FAQs - Earthquakes**
   Q: I was born and raised in South Bend, Indiana and I remember experiencing a tremor on a Fall Saturday, right about mid-day, sometime between 1968 and...
   http://www.indiana.edu/~igs/faqs/faqquake.html - size 3K - 15-Jul-97 - English

2. **Index of /ftp/ca.earthquakes/1994/**
   Index of /ftp/ca.earthquakes/1994/ Name Last modified Size Description. Parent Directory 30-Jan-97 10:35 - 940106.gif 16-Nov-94 14:18 11K. 940106.ps.Z...
   http://scec.gps.caltech.edu/ftp/ca.earthquakes/1994/ - size 21K - 15-Aug-97 - English

3. **Index of /ftp/ca.earthquakes/1993/**
   Index of /ftp/ca.earthquakes/1993/ Name Last modified Size Description. Parent Directory 30-Jan-97 10:35 - 930107.ps.Z 08-Aug-94 10:17 40K. 930107.txt.Z...
   http://scec.gps.caltech.edu/ftp/ca.earthquakes/1993/ - size 18K - 15-Aug-97 - English

4. **USENET FAQs - sci.geo.earthquakes**
   USENET FAQs. sci.geo.earthquakes. FAQs in this newsgroup. Satellite Imagery FAQ - Pointer.
   http://www.cis.ohio-state.edu/hypertext/faq/usenet-faqs/bygroup/sci/geo/earthquakes/top.html - size 328 bytes - 15-Aug-97 - English

5. **GEOL 240lxg: Earthquakes**
   GEOL 240lxg: Earthquakes. Department: Earth Sciences. Instructor: Sammis, Charles & Teng, Ta-Liang. Semester offered: Fall Spring. Category: Natural...
   http://www.usc.edu/Library/Gede/GEOL240lxg.SammisCharles.html - size 2K - 22-Nov-95 - English

Grouping Operators

- The grouping **operators** join words and phrases together to be treated as a single unit or determine the order in which Boolean operators are applied.

- The most common grouping operators are:

Double quotes   The documents found in the search must contain the words inside double quotes exactly as entered. For example, a search for "*World Wide Web*" will find sites whose descriptions contain the phrase *World Wide Web*, not the individual words separated by other words or the same words uncapitalized.

Parentheses   Words and operators can be grouped to refine searches using parentheses or to define the order in which Boolean operators are applied. For example, a search for (*Internet OR Web*) AND *browser* will find sites whose descriptions contain the words *Internet* and *browser* or *Web* and *browser*. (Note that this is *not* the same search as *Internet* OR *Web AND browser*, which finds sites whose descriptions contain either the word *Internet* or both of the words *Web* and *browser*.)

Case Sensitive

- If you enter a word using all lowercase (hamlet), some search engines will look for both upper and lower case versions of the word. If you use uppercase in the search (Hamlet), the search engine will locate documents that only use the uppercase version.

Special Characters and Punctuation

- Special characters and punctuation can also be used to filter results in complex searches. The most widely used character, the asterisk (*) is used when a word in a search can have a number of different forms. Using the asterisk (*) as a wildcard tells the search engine to find documents that contain any form of the word. For example, if you create a search for blue*, note the wide range of documents that show up in the search results.

Click to find related books at **Amazon.com**.
About **800775** documents match your query.

1. Yahoo! - U.S. blue chips slash losses, Nasdaq edges higher
   Yahoo | Write Us | Search | Headlines | Info] [Business - Company - Industry - Finance - PR Newswire - Business Wire - Quotes] Thursday August 14 3:20..
   http://biz.yahoo.com/finance/97/08/14/z0000_21.html - size 4K - 15-Aug-97 - English

2. SI: BLUE DESERT MINING, BDE-ASE
   BLUE DESERT MINING, BDE-ASE. Carlson On-line Profile | Started By: Dale Schwartzenhauer Date: Mar 9 1997 12:52AM EST. Investors should check out BDE, one..
   http://www.techstocks.com/~wsapi/investor/Subject-13562 - size 4K - 15-Aug-97 - English

3. UBL Artist: Daly Planet Blues Band
   Daly Planet Blues Band. The Daly Planet home page The only resource for info on this jam band from Hilton Head Island, SC. Band info, pictures, contact...
   http://www.ubl.com/artists/009821.html - size 6K - 7-Aug-97 - English

4. takuroku blues
   http://www.sainet.or.jp/~akihisa/ - size 242 bytes - 16-Feb-97

5. From Deep Blue to deep space: Take a panoramic look at Mars' surface
   Take a panoramic look at Mars' surface. To view the image* below, you'll need to install IBM's PanoramIX plug-in for the Netscape Navigator browser. The...
   http://www.ibm.com/Stories/1997/07/space6.html - size 2K - 30-Jul-97 - English

---

- Wildcards are useful if you are looking for a word that could be singular or plural (look for dog*, instead of dog to broaden the search results).

- Other characters that can help limit, filter, and sort results include: %, $, !, | (called the piping symbol), ~ (called the tilde), < (less than), and > (greater than). Check the rules of the individual search engines to see how, or if, these characters can be used.

Major Search Engines and Operators

■ Below is a table of the major search tools and how they use some of the search operators. Be sure to check out the search tips and help sections of the sites that you use frequently to see the most current search options. Search tools are constantly updating and improving their sites in response to users' needs.

Search Tool	Boolean operators	+/−	Grouping Operators	Case Sensitivity
AltaVista	✓	✓	✓	✓
AOL NetFind	✓	✓		
Excite	✓	✓	✓	
HotBot	✓	✓	✓	✓
Infoseek		✓	✓	✓
Lycos		✓	✓	
SavvySearch		✓	✓	
Yahoo	✓	✓	✓	✓

WEB RESOURCES

Use General Sites

◆ **America Online** ◆ **Microsoft Network** ◆ **Pathfinder**

General sites such as America Online and Microsoft Network have become much more than gateways to the World Wide Web. The best of these sites offer rich online content that can eliminate the need to surf and search the sometimes confusing and tangled Web.

At these general sites you can find the day's news, weather, sports, opinion, special interest features, and in some cases travel services, entertainment reviews, and other specialty information. Some sites also offer you the option of tailoring the home page to suit your personal needs.

These sites are bound to improve as they compete for additional subscribers with more and better content. Take advantage of these sites to get a great start to your Web experience every time you log online.

America Online

http://www.aol.com

 The home page for the leading commercial online service provides a well-organized directory of links to dozens of top Web sites along with brief reviews of each site.

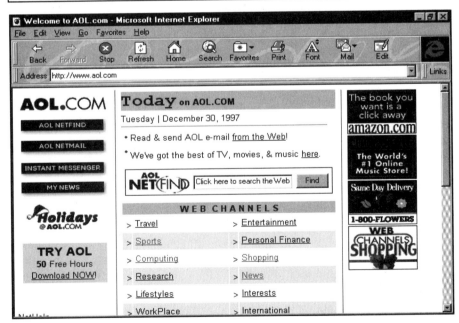

- The AOL Web site isn't just for Internet newcomers and home Web surfers. This site provides a good jumping-off point for any practical Web search.

- The AOL site has a comprehensive and well-organized Web directory, with access to dozens of links to many of the best resources available on the Web. Just click one of the AOL channels to see links to Web sites that AOL has selected as favorites along with a brief descriptive paragraph about each site.

- Though most of the channels are primarily oriented to a consumer audience, you can click the WorkPlace channel to see a very complete directory of business Web site links and associated site reviews.

- A few of the selected favorites on each channel are links to an AOL service available only to AOL members, but you will find many more links to sites available to you on the Web.

- A selection of AOL Web site reviews is arranged at the left side of each channel page. Click one of the review topics to dig down deeper and find more Web site links.

- Another nice feature at the AOL site is the easy access to search engine text boxes, where you can quickly enter a keyword search topic and click to find what you need. Each AOL channel typically showcases two or three Web sites near the top of the channel page by including search engine text boxes for those sites.

- Click the NetFind link to use the very helpful Time Savers directory. Here you will find links Web resources for many common tasks such as Find an Airline or Hotel, Plan a Night Out, Plan a Night In, Manage Your Investments, Your Health, and Your Government.

- Links to AOL services such as NetMail (Web access e-mail) and Instant Messenger are also featured at the AOL site, but you must be an AOL member to use these services.

Microsoft Network

http://www.msn.com

 This leading computer software developer provides a broad range of online content for business and consumer research as well as entertainment.

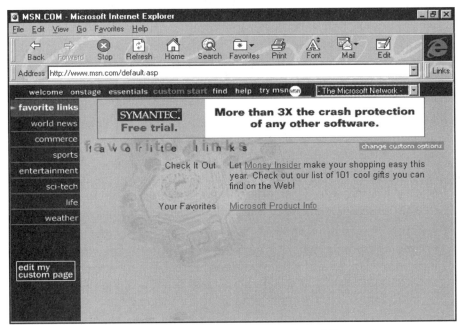

- There has been a pattern over the years when Microsoft enters a promising new market: Microsoft may not offer the first or best product, but after a while, the Microsoft product catches on and then overtakes the competition.

- The same pattern holds true in the commercial online service market. Microsoft Network (MSN) was supposed to take over the world when it was offered as an icon on the Windows 95 desktop several years ago. However, as many people who clicked the icon on their desktop found, the initial content available on MSN usually wasn't worth a second look. In addition, the network connections were typically slow and unreliable.

- Over the past couple of years, MSN's content has vastly improved, even if the network connections remain slow at times. MSN's wide range of consumer and business Web site offerings makes it well worth a stop on your online search.

- Topping the list of MSN sites is the award winning Expedia travel service. (See "Plan and Book Travel Online.") Expedia is an example of how much interactivity and rich content can be delivered on a commercial Web site. Expedia's outstanding travel-booking wizard makes it a fine business and sales resource. Sidewalk is a wonderfully complete guide to nine U.S. cities as well as Sydney, Australia.

- Check out Microsoft Investor and Money Insider for a couple of the best investment and market sites available on the Web. Also, try the Computing Central site for computer forums, tips, software downloads, and industry news.

- The Mining Company is a new search site offered by MSN that offers the services of online guides to help you find what you want. Other MSN sites are consumer-oriented, but provide very useful and well-presented resources to help you find out about cars (CarPoint), movies (Cinemania), games (Internet Gaming Zone), music (Music Central), and shopping (Plaza).

Pathfinder

http://pathfinder.com

 Use this easy-to-access directory to find Time Warner media Web sites such as Time, Life, People, Fortune, CNNSI, and Travel & Leisure. Perhaps the most complete and wide-ranging collection of current information available on the Web.

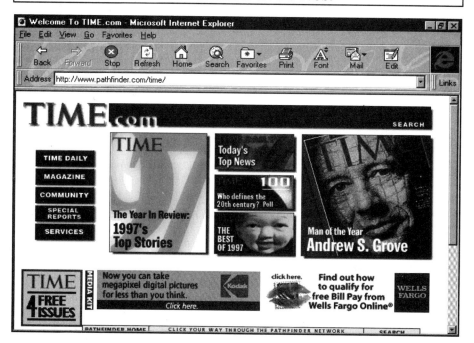

- Time Warner's Pathfinder site brings together all the news, information, and entertainment content of dozens of Web, magazine, and video properties owned by the media conglomerate.

- This site is a great source for news, sports, politics, and entertainment coverage, offering links to Time, CNNSI, People, Entertainment Weekly, Variety Netwire, Life, and AllPolitics.

- The above list is just a sampling of the interesting and informative resources available at Pathfinder. You can also find financial sites such as Fortune, Hoover's Business Resources, Money Daily, Money Online, Portfolio Tracker, and Quick Quotes.

- Get travel news and fares at the Travel & Leisure, WebFlyer, PlanetSurfer, and Magellan Maps sites. Net Culture sites feature PC and Web news and information.

- If you want to shop, click on one of the many Marketplace sites, including BarnesandNoble.com, CDNow, Fortune Book Fair, Internet Shopping Network, and Time Life Photo Sight.

- Pathfinder also provides free e-mail service, a financial calculator, community chat sites, a cyberdating service, and an investment portfolio tracker. This wide-ranging collection of sites may be one of the most comprehensive information sources available on the Web.

Use Directories and Search Engines

◆ **Yahoo!** ◆ **Excite** ◆ **Dogpile** ◆ **Open Text** ◆ **Other Sites**

If you're using the Internet for business, your main objective for being online is most likely to find a particular piece of information. Although it can be a lot of fun, you don't want to waste time surfing the Web.

When you want information on the Web fast but don't know where to look, the best place to start is a directory or search engine. These sites help organize the vast contents of the Internet and the World Wide Web so that you can focus your search efforts and zoom to the exact Web site (or other Internet service) you need.

Directories Organize the Web

- Though they go about it in different ways, directories and search engines have the same goal—locating information online. Directories provide a map of how information is organized on the World Wide Web. Typically, they break the Web down into a number of categories—usually numbering about a dozen or so.

- Categories might include broad search areas such as Arts and Humanities, Business, Computers and Internet, News and Media, Science, and Entertainment. Beyond the main categories, directories typically break Web contents down into finer and finer subcategories. For example, the Business category might be split into Companies, Investing, Classifieds, Taxes, and more. Searching these layers of subcategories until you find what you need is called "drilling down" in the directory.

Search Engines Comb the Web

- Search engines provide you with readily accessible database search software that searches Web contents or, in some cases, directories or indexes of Web contents. You enter one or more keywords into the search engine's text box, click a button on screen, and then let the software do the work.

- Typically, a search engine will return a listing of results that match your keyword(s) as closely as possible. Many search engines include confidence rankings that indicate how closely the software thinks each result matches your keyword(s). Results may be links to Web sites or links to directory categories or subcategories.

- Search Web sites can include directories, search engines, or both. They may also contain news updates and other content found only at the search site. Each of these sites finds information on the Web differently, and that can help you find what you need faster once you have learned the unique benefits of each site's approach.

Yahoo!

http://www.yahoo.com

 Yahoo!, the original Web search site, provides a well-organized directory of Web contents, a powerful search engine, and an ever-growing list of new features that focus on special interests.

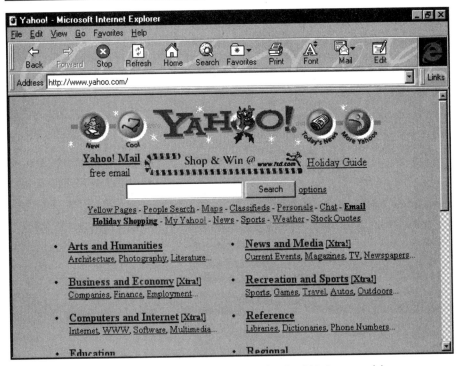

- Perhaps the most recognizable name in the Web searching business is Yahoo!, the granddaddy of them all. The site is continuously updated and new Yahoo! services are added regularly to expand the site. Click on the New icon at the top of the home page to see what features have been added recently.

- What Yahoo! does best is organize the Web. The list of directory categories and subcategories on the Yahoo! home page has been emulated by many other Web search and directory sites. If you have a fairly good idea of what you're looking for, click the category (or subcategory) link that comes closest to matching your interest.

- After clicking a category link, you will see a page of subcategory links. Click one of these to drill down even further in the directory structure and narrow your search. After two or three clicks, you should start to zero in on links to specific Web sites.

- You can also click on the Indices link after you have clicked a top-level category link to see a listing of Web sites that serve as link directories for that particular topic. For example, click Business and Economy, then click Indices to see links to sites such as All Business Network, Business Sense, and Business Sources on the Net.

- From the Yahoo! home page you can also click Today's News icon for a quick way to check the day's headlines. Click the More Yahoos icon to see a listing of other Yahoo! services such as My Yahoo! (where you can customize the site to your liking), Get Local (focusing on a Zip Code you specify), Yahoo! Chat (for online talk), and various Yahoo! Metros (focusing on major cities across the country). Click the home page Cool icon to see a directory of more off-the-wall Web site categories.

- You can also search the Yahoo! directories by entering a keyword(s) in the search text boxes available on every page. You can search the entire Yahoo! directory or limit the search to the portion you're currently visiting. Remember, Yahoo! searches only its directories, which consist of Web page titles and descriptions, not the full Web. This yields more focused search results.

Excite

http://www.excite.com

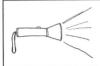 Excite features a tight directory structure and allows searching by concepts, which means you can enter conversational search phrases and get more targeted results.

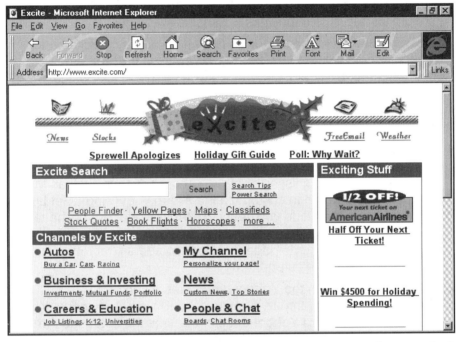

- After trying a few keyword searches, you may come to discover that Web search engines take your keywords very literally. The Excite Web site attempts to solve this problem by enabling you to search by concepts instead of by keywords.

- That is, the Excite search engine knows that words such as "coffee" and "cake" can have different meanings when they are used together from when they are used separately. The Excite engine also knows that words such as "play" can have many meanings, and it takes these into account when you enter a concept phrase.

- The bottom line is that you can use conversational phrases to describe what you want Excite to find. For example, if you're looking for plays by Arthur Miller, just type in "plays by Arthur Miller." If you're looking for sports plays of the day, just type in "sports plays of the day." Excite eliminates the process of deciding what the best keyword strategy will be to get the search results you want.

- Excite also provides a very tight Web directory that includes only three levels of categories. This is a reflection of the more narrow criteria Excite uses to screen sites indexed in its directory.

- You are guaranteed to find links to Web sites by the time you click three Excite category links. You can also read Excite summaries of each site that links to it. The net result for you is a quicker, more informed directory search than you can perform at other directory sites.

- Excite also includes links to features such as News (well-organized directory of wire service reports), Stocks (a business news summary page with stock quotes), TV (a table-style television guide), and Weather (national and local forecasts).

Dogpile

http://www.dogpile.com

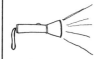 Use this search engine of search engines to look for what you want on 25 Internet search and directory sites.

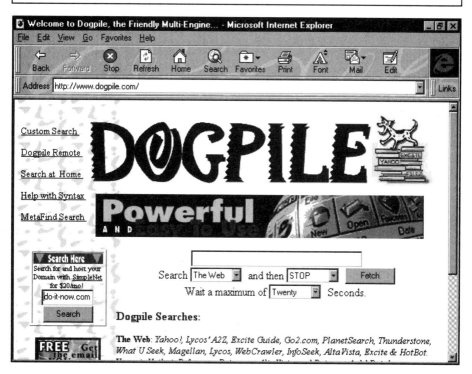

- Want to get the maximum coverage for your search? If you have trouble finding results at one search or directory site and have to jump to another, try Dogpile instead. Dogpile is the Internet search site that checks all the other important search and directory sites.

- You can enter a keyword search into the Dogpile home page and specify whether you want Dogpile to search the Web, FTP, Usenet, or newswires. You can choose to search a maximum of two of the above and then select a maximum time you want to wait for the search to be completed.

- Click the Fetch button and the powerful Dogpile search engine begins searching your selected Internet services three at a time. Dogpile searches 25 different services, including Yahoo!, Excite, Lycos, WebCrawler, InfoSeek, AltaVista, HotBot, DejaNews, and more. You can rest assured that you have thoroughly combed the Internet after finishing a Dogpile search.

- You can also specify the order in which you want Dogpile to search by clicking on the Custom Search link. Just select the service you want to search for each spot on the Dogpile search list from 1 to 25.

- Click on the Help with Syntax link to read a detailed how-to page for using keyword search operators such as AND, OR, NOT, and NEAR. Because some search engines support these keyword operators in different ways, you should check out the Help with Syntax page before constructing any complex Dogpile searches.

Open Text

http://index.opentext.net

 Search every word of the World Wide Web with the Open Text engine.

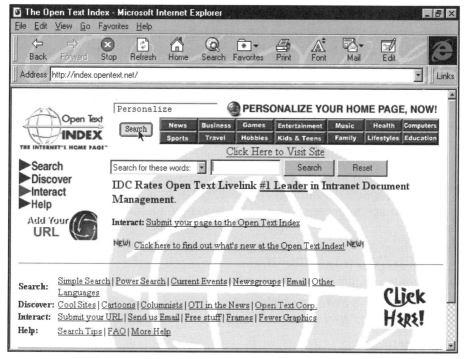

- When you really want to search the entire World Wide Web, use the Open Text search engine. Open Text treats the Web as one gigantic text file. Your keyword search in Open Text is virtually the same as using the Find feature in a word processing document, but in this case the document is the Web.

- From the Open Text index page, enter your keyword search in the text box. Click on the search button and wait for a results page to appear.

- Typically, you will get a large number of pages that match your search keyword(s). You can narrow the search by clicking the Power Search link. On the Power Search page you can enter multiple search keywords (one per text box), select where you want to search (narrow the search to titles, summaries, first headings, or

URLs), and link the keywords with search operators such as and, or, but not, near, or followed by.

- Drop-down list menus in Power Search provide choices for search locations and operators to make selection easier. Remember that the more keywords you use, the narrower your search will be (unless you connect the words with or, which includes all the keywords).

- You can also search current events, e-mail, newsgroups, and other languages. With a little practice and experimentation, Open Text searches can yield pleasantly surprising and highly effective search results.

Other Sites

Infoseek

http://www.infoseek.com

- Search any part of the Web quickly and easily with this widely respected search and directory page. It is easy to perform quick searches as well more complex searches at this site.

Lycos

http://www.lycos.com

- This full-featured search and directory site is famous for its top 5% reviews of Web sites. Its high-powered Custom Search page lets you hone in on the results you need.

DejaNews

http://www.dejanews.com

- This site searches Usenet newsgroups, the Internet's version of online chat bulletin boards. Handy for finding experts on a particular topic or just tapping into a discussion about a subject of interest.

The Mining Company

http://www.miningcompany.com

- This site takes a unique approach to finding information on the Web, with special interest sections led by "Guides" who specialize in a particular topic area. The Guide points you to links of interest, and you can also search the site by interest areas, subsections, or related sites.

Check Business News

◆ **BusinessWeek Online** ◆ **Forbes Digital Tool** ◆ **Journal of Commerce** ◆ **Upside.Com** ◆ **Other Sites**

Check these sites to get a handle on business news and trends. Though there are a multitude of online sites for business magazines, journals, and newspapers, all the sites featured here combine complete coverage, timely updates, and in-depth reporting. Features and opinion pieces provide you with expert analysis to aid in business decision making.

BusinessWeek Online

http://www.businessweek.com

 The online home of this top business weekly magazine provides in-depth coverage of the week's events as well as a complete daily business news update.

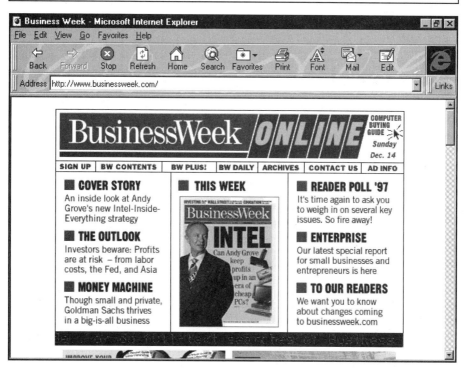

- BusinessWeek is a leading source of information for business people, and its online site delivers all the information you will find in the weekly magazine and then some. Though all of the BusinessWeek site is available online free of charge at the time of this writing, the editors of the magazine have announced that there will be a subscription fee starting in January 1998.

- The home page features articles from the current week's edition of the magazine. Click the picture of the magazine's cover to see a complete directory of links to the issue's contents.

- Click the BW Daily link to get a complete look at the day's business news at the Daily Briefing page. The Daily Briefing includes numerous in-depth articles produced by BusinessWeek and Standard & Poor's.

- Click on the BW Plus link to access several months' worth of archived articles on topics such as the best business schools, business books online, The Computer Room, Enterprise Online for entrepreneurs and small business owners, Investor's Central, and Personal Business.

Forbes Digital Tool

http://www.forbes.com

 Irreverent approach to commentary on the world of business makes this site a can't-miss resource.

- Forbes Magazine has long been noted for a somewhat irreverent mix of business news reporting and opinionated features and opinion pieces. You can browse the content of five Forbes publications online at the Forbes Digital Tool Web site.

- Publications available online include the original Forbes Magazine, Forbes ASAP (focused on the impact of technology in business), Forbes FYI (features, entertainment, and opinion), American Heritage (a lively magazine about American history), and the Gilder Telecosm Series (articles excerpted from the book Telecosm, which examines and predicts trends in the online world).

- As if access to all of these publications were not enough, you can also click on the Toolbox icon to use the many Forbes lists of corporations and business people (such as The 500 Largest Private Companies in the US and Corporate America's Most Powerful People), Digital Tool Databases (such as a New York dining guide and a fitness guide), cool software downloads (such as the NBD Daily Rocket Investment Monitor), and a couple of nifty financial calculators.

- You can also click the On My Mind icon to participate in an active and entertaining online forum. The Forbes Toolbox is available free of charge, for the moment at least, so stop here to get business news and views with a healthy dose of attitude.

Journal of Commerce

http://www.joc.com

 Hardcore news, facts, and figures about the marketplace, commodities, trade, and transportation.

- The Journal of Commerce (JOC) Web site keeps you up to date with trade, transportation, and global market news.
- The site has a tight focus on domestic and international commerce, including in-depth information on transportation, logistics, imports and exports, foreign markets, energy, insurance, and finance. You can also find professional reporting unique to the Journal of Commerce site on electronic communications, chemicals, and commodities.
- Check the JOC home page for commerce headlines, summaries, and links to full stories. Click the JOC News icon to go to a directory of links to top commerce news stories. Major news categories include Page One, Trade, Transportation, Insurance, Energy/Commodities, and Opinion. These links can also be found on the home page.
- You can also click to find oil prices, shipping schedules, and transportation data. The JOC is by far the most complete site for tracking the nuts and bolts of commerce and trade.

Upside.Com

http://www.upside.com

 The Upside.com site helps provide perspective on developments in business and technology.

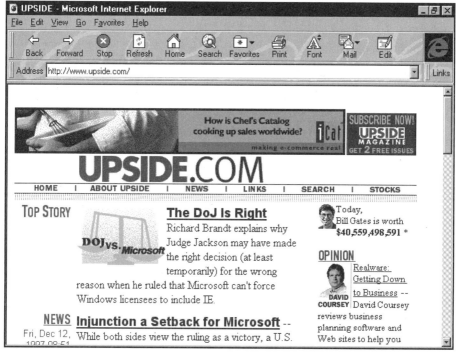

- Upside is a business magazine that focuses on industries that use and develop digital technology. The Upside.com Web site features the magazine's editorial content plus daily news updates, a technology stock watch that tracks long-term performance, as well as other tools for managers involved in the business of technology.

- Daily tech news headlines are featured at the site home page. Click the News link to scan the full text of the daily news articles. Click Links to access a number of other helpful business sites.

- The most valuable part of the Upside.com site is perhaps the wealth of insightful opinion pieces available. Click on Opinion to see a complete listing of recent columns and links to archives of past issues. The columns here are an indispensable resource for understanding the evolving future of business and technology.

Other Sites

Wall Street Journal Interactive

http://interactive.wsj.com

- For about $50 a year you get complete Wall Street Journal coverage online plus Barron's online market commentary, the SmartMoney Interactive online investment planning service, and the Briefing Book company reports database.

Inc. Online

http://www.inc.com

- The online version of Inc. magazine has been awarded the Folio editorial excellence award for best online magazine of the year. Go here for excellent features about what it takes to run a successful business and some powerful interactive worksheets that can help you analyze your company's performance.

Fast Company

http://www.fastcompany.com/today/central.html

- Innovative Web site that aspires to provide a handbook for the changing business world of new technology, global markets, and independent agents who have given up the corporate world to strike out on their own. News and features address issues for the self-employed and entrepreneurs to help smooth out the bumps in the road to success.

Red Herring

http://www.herring.com

- Another top site for business technology news and features, Red Herring also covers the business of entertainment. True to its name, Red Herring seeks to provide insight that takes you beyond technology marketing hype.

Receive Custom Information from Push Channels

◆ **PointCast** ◆ **Marimba Castanet** ◆ **NewsHound** ◆ **Other Sites**

Push technology has received a lot of press coverage in the past year as the next, or perhaps first, "killer application" for the World Wide Web. The idea is to have a customized selection of "channels" that deliver a steady stream of information to your computer's desktop over the Internet.

While the idea of having continuously and readily available information on your computer about topics of interest to you may sound like a good one, some drawbacks still exist, primarily due to the speed limitations of sending "live" information over the Internet and the fact that a stream of incoming data can slow computers and networks to a crawl.

Still, there are some definite advantages to tailoring news and information from the Web to fit your needs. The sites listed here take somewhat different approaches to delivering the information to you, using more or less intrusive means of giving you what you want. Take your hardware system and your information needs into consideration when deciding which of these services is the right one for you.

If you get ambitious, you can even use sites such as PointCast and Marimba Castanet to publish your own push channel information.

PointCast

http://www.pointcast.com

Use this top push service to get news and business information from sources you choose delivered directly to your desktop.

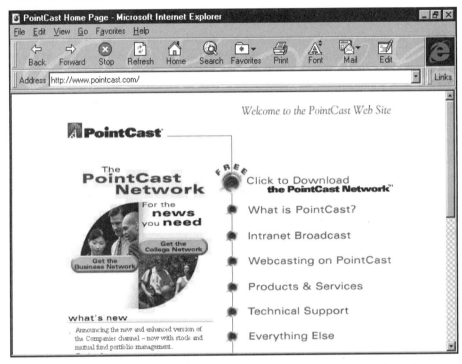

- Use the PointCast network to have information you want downloaded to your desktop automatically. The PointCast newscast gathers stories from a wide range of sources and presents them to your desktop using tickers and "smartscreens" that flash on your desktop.

- PointCast has received a lot of rave reviews over the past year for being a screen saver that keeps you on top of your world. It can, however, create information overload. Also, be aware that using PointCast can really slow down your network or computer.

- Click to read a full story or customize the channels you want to see. You can have PointCast continually update if you're directly connected to the Internet, or you can schedule times for PointCast to log on and update automatically.

- Use the Business Network to focus on daily business news. Track firms in your investment portfolio or competing companies via the Companies channel. You can also create your own push channel for broadcast on the Web using PointCast Connections.

Marimba Castanet

http://www.marimba.com

 Use Marimba Castanet to publish and to receive push channel information. Marimba's publishing tools make creating your own push channel fairly painless.

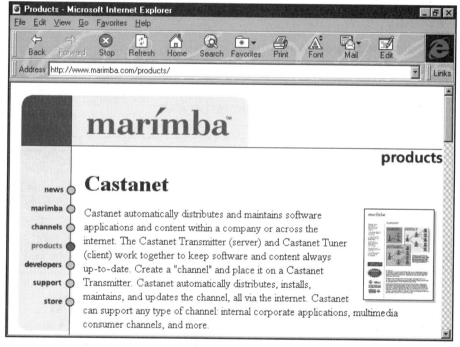

- Marimba Castanet is another popular push service that lets you download various Castanet channels of your choice and then have those channels automatically update with fresh information. You can also choose to update each time you log on to the Internet if you're not directly connected.

- Choose the channels you want to use and then customize these channels to your liking. Once you download the Castanet Tuner to your computer, you can choose any channel you want from the Castanet Transmitter.

- Channels update automatically (even when you are offline) and transmit only new information to improve the speed with which the information downloads. Once you add a channel to your computer, it is always available, whether or not you are online. You can even access the channel from your laptop while traveling and away from a network connection.

- You can also publish your own channel with Castanet fairly easily. In simplest terms, the process involves uploading the files you want to include for broadcast to the Castanet Transmitter server. Publishing it on the Transmitter server makes it available to Castanet clients as a channel that will be updated automatically on their computers each time you make a change to the channel content.

NewsHound

http://www.newshound.com

Use a trainable search agent to track down news and information from the Web.

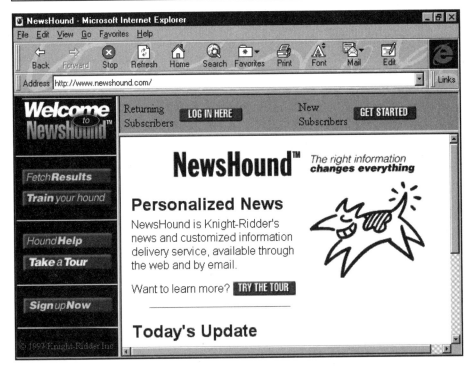

- If you want to have a push site actually track down information on the Web about a particular topic you're interested in, NewsHound delivers the goods.

- A service of the Knight-Ridder newspaper chain, NewsHound tracks and delivers up to five news or information topics for about $8 per month.

- To use NewsHound, sign up for the basic service, then "train" your NewsHounds to search for the information you want. The NewsHound service will then keep an eye out for stories and Web information that fit your search profile, gather anything that matches, and send it to your machine either in Web or e-mail format.

- This is a great way to keep tabs on a particular company, market, or developing news or technology story without the intrusiveness and system slow-downs of other push services.

Other Sites

Headliner

http://www.headliner.com

- This news and information ticker service slows your machine with a lot of graphics. However, Headliner is not as intrusive as some of the better known services such as PointCast.

Infobeat

http://www.infobeat.com

- Infobeat provides another way to avoid slowing your desktop with information you may not need. With Infobeat, you select the type of "Beats" you want to keep track of, including Finance, Sports, News, Weather, Entertainment, and more. Then Infobeat sends you personalized e-mail updates on the topics you choose.

CNN Custom News

http://www.cnn.com

- Tailor news delivery from CNN by clicking on the Custom News icon at the CNN home page. You can create a custom user profile to have news, sports scores, stock tickers—whatever information is important to you—delivered to your desktop. You can build your own profile or choose from among six Quickstart profiles including A Little of Everything, US & World News, Business, Science & Technology, Sports, as well as Lifestyle & Showbiz.

Find Technology News

◆ CNET ◆ Dataquest ◆ ZDNet ◆ AltaVista ◆ Other Sites

Learn the latest technology news by checking these sites. Each site includes in-depth feature articles on what the future holds in various segments of the computer industry as well as breaking stories about innovations that can help your business.

There are many places to learn about computer and technology news on the Web. Nearly every general news and directory site includes a full slate of technology news updates each day. The sites covered here stand out, however, because technology is their primary focus.

CNET

http://www.cnet.com

 Keep up-to-date on technology information with this top site for computer news. Articles are entertaining and include numerous links to other tech sites.

132

- CNET Central is a popular cable television show featuring news about cutting edge technology delivered in a friendly, entertaining format. The CNET Web site essentially follows suit. Here you can find great features about the latest innovations in information technology presented in a style that will appeal to the everyday user as well as the certified technogeek.

- The CNET home page includes links to articles on the day's top tech news as well as links to a multitude of very detailed product performance tests, reviews, and comparisons. Examples of recent product reviews include "Ten Bargain ISPs (Internet Service Providers) Compared," "Six Laser Printers for Under $400," and "Notebooks Under $2,500: CNET Reviews Nine Portable PCs You Can Afford."

- Click the CNET TV link to get information about the various CNET television shows, including the original CNET Central, The Web, The New Edge, and Tech Reports, which are brief tech news updates broadcast on local TV news programs.

- The Software Central page includes indexes of software ranked according to popularity (based on the number of copies downloaded from the CNET site), CNET editors' picks, and newest titles. This is a convenient place to see what's new and download it.

- The CNET SERVICES section includes several useful links such as Shareware.com, where you can find hundreds of shareware titles, and News.com, where a more complete listing of the day's tech news appears.

- The MARKETPLACE section includes links such as Buydirect.com, where you can purchase almost any type of software direct from the manufacturer, as well as a list of Specials, which are discount software deals culled from the Buydirect site.

- The Features section includes a wide range of "How To" articles, an entertaining set of articles called Digital Life, and a more expert-oriented set of articles called Techno. A recent check of the Digital Life section turned up entertaining columns titled "Ten technologies that will never work" and "Eight myths about the millenium bug." Among the ten technologies supposed to be going nowhere: Internet "Push" technology, ISDN lines, and the $500 Network PC. You may not agree with the predictions, but this is the kind of cutting edge tech talk that you will find regularly at the CNET site.

Dataquest

http://www.dataquest.com

This site posts corporate information, technology research, news, and analysis. The Gartner Group produces the Dataquest page, which features articles about latest tech trends which features. You must be a Gartner Group client to access more in-depth reports.

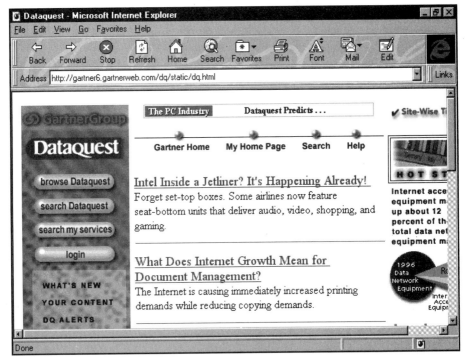

- Make time for a quick stop at the Dataquest page to get a briefing on what the Dataquest and Gartner Group analysts predict as trends to watch for in the PC Industry. You can view tech news and analysis headlines and click links to read brief associated articles. However, you can't access Dataquest statistics and analysis unless you're a registered Gartner Group user.

- Don't let the limited access deter you from visiting this site. A quick scan of the analysis and trends covered here can provide valuable insight into the business of information technology.

ZDNet

http://www.zdnet.com

 This is a very comprehensive technology news site with an attitude somewhere between the hip CNET and the buttoned-down corporate approach at Dataquest.

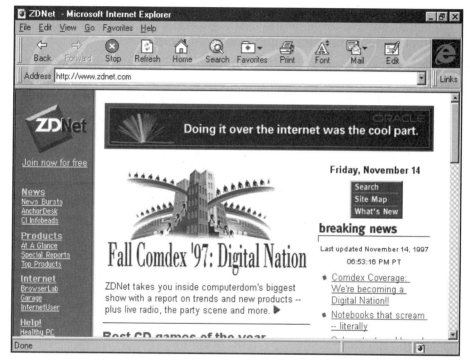

- The ZDNet site, run by Ziff-Davis, Inc., publishers of PC Magazine, PC Week, PC Computing, and Computer Shopper, among others, is a great place to search and access the content and resources of all these publications. With many of the most respected technology publications and columnists in the fold, this is perhaps the best site to find the latest computer news and opinions.

- The ZDNet home page features the latest computer news headlines. Click on News links to find News Bursts, AnchorDesk, and CI Infobeads. News Bursts includes the latest computer news headlines. AnchorDesk is a source for industry opinion with a bit of a chip on its shoulder. The CI Infobeads link takes you to the Computer Intelligence InfoBeads site, where you can find a wealth of Information Technology industry data and statistics.

- Almost every section of the ZDNet site includes a search feature to help you find information for the exact topic you want.

- The Products links provide you with one of the top computer hardware and software product review resources on the Web. Click on Reviews at a Glance to see a list of links to ZDNet reviews organized by product category. Special Reports provide a more detailed look at specific products, including beta previews and opinion pieces for products such as Windows 98. Product Awards is a clearinghouse for all of the many awards bestowed upon computer products by ZD publications editors.

- Internet links provide how-to Web user and developer resources, including The Garage, which features a selection of how-to articles for those interested in do-it-yourself Web page construction.

- Finally, the Help! Channel links may in fact be the best reason to visit ZDNet. The Help! Channel Healthy PC links include useful resources such as The Tip Zone, where you can enter a topic and search for tips and answers, Fix It Now!, Free Downloads for shareware, and an Ask the Experts section where you can consult with PC power users. Other gems include Online Video Demos and the Support Finder index of links to vender tech support sites.

AltaVista

http://www.altavista.com

 Good technology information site, but less comprehensive than others and colored somewhat by the fact that it is run by Digital Equipment Corporation, a computer hardware manufacturer.

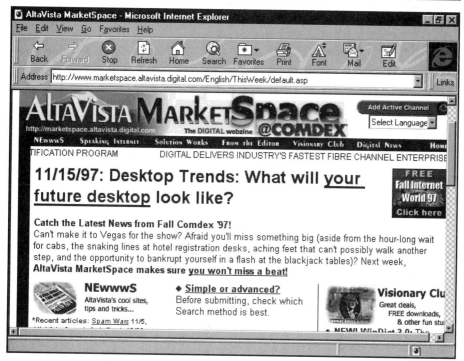

- AltaVista was a fairly early entry into the Web search and news site category, and while there is still a lot of great in-depth tech industry reporting on this site, it's not as comprehensive as either the CNET or ZDNet sites.

- Also, the fact that the site is run by a major corporate player in the industry should give you reason to pause before assuming that you're getting a complete picture of what's new and where the tech industry is headed. A somewhat annoying ticker of Digital corporate news at the top of the home page is a prominent example of the bias in coverage.

- Still, there is enough here to merit a visit and search every now and then, especially if you're looking for information about a specific topic and haven't been able to find it elsewhere.

Other Sites

Wired

http://www.hotwired.com/frontdoor/

- Cutting-edge tech news delivered with a Generation X attitude.

Emmerce

http://www.computerworld.com/emmerce/index.html

- Part of the Computerworld news magazine site, this Web magazine focuses on the emerging field of electronic commerce.

Internet News.com

http://www.internetnews.com

- A down-to-business look at Internet trends and news. An excellent resource for companies developing Internet technology and commerce.

Intranet Journal

http://www.intranetjournal.com

- The ultimate source for news and information for IT executives charged with developing and managing a corporate intranet.

Research Business, Finance, and Economic Trends

◆ **Media Logic** ◆ **StatUSA** ◆ **Financial Data Finder** ◆ **Other Sites**

Keep an eye on the current economic and financial climate and get a glimpse of what the future holds by checking the wealth of information in these sites. At these sites you can obtain data and statistics for a vast number of macroeconomic indicators, as well as industry and commerce trends.

Media Logic

http://www.mlinet.com

 A treasure trove of reports, data, and statistics for big picture economic trends.

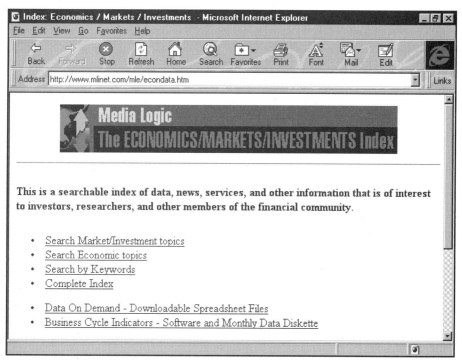

- Where can you find a link to almost any type of economic, market, and investment information? One place: The Media Logic Web site.

- The Media Logic home page includes links to stock market and investment topics, economic topics, business cycle indicators, and Data on Demand economic spreadsheets.

- Click on the Complete Index link to search the complete site. From the Contents page you can select whether you want to search by topic or by information type.

- Topics include Market and Investment, General Economics, and Business and Economic Indicators.

- Information types include Company/Organization Home Pages, Data, News, On-Line Services, Brokers, Articles & Documentation, Software, Stores, and Indices.

- For example, clicking on General Economic Topics opens a page from which you can select various sectors of the economy, including Manufacturing, Agriculture, Business, Consumer, Government, General, and Other.

- The following illustration shows an example of the links that appear when you click the Business Sector link. As you can see, this is a gold mine of economic and business data.

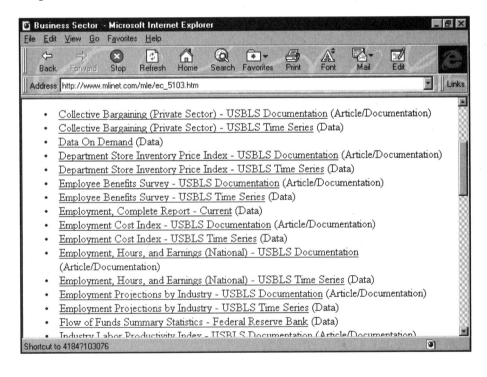

StatUSA

http://www.stat-usa.gov/

 U.S. Department of Commerce reports and statistics for major economic indicators.

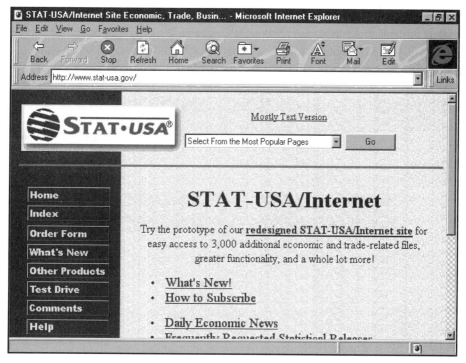

- Where do you go to find the statistical data behind the news soundbyte reports about the nation's leading economic indicators? The Department of Commerce regularly releases reports such as Housing Starts, Manufacturing Inventory and Sales, and Advance Retail Sales.

- These reports are used to monitor and forecast the health of the economy. Through the StatUSA site you can access the data and use it to help make strategic business decisions.

- Click on Frequently Requested Statistical Releases to see reports on leading economic indicators, fiscal and monetary reports, financial market statistics, price, productivity, industrial, and labor statistics, as well as regional economic statistics.

- Click on Daily Economic News to get up-to-the-minute Commerce Department reports such as bond rates, foreign exchange rates, and the Daily Treasury Statement.

- Though you must subscribe to the service to gain access to the data and reports, the charge is minimal (approximately $150/year or $50/quarter) and well worth the amount of economic information available.

Financial Data Finder

http://www.cob.ohio-state.edu/dept/fin/osudata.htm

 Outstanding directory containing dozens of links to financial and business Web sites.

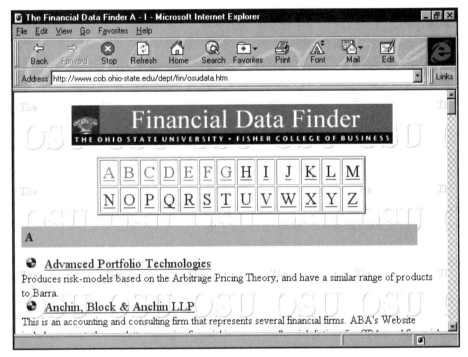

- Ohio State University's Fisher College of Business maintains one of the most complete collections of links to business and finance Web pages at the Financial Data Finder. More than just a college grad student project, this site is a valuable resource for any executive who needs to locate business information and online financial resources.

- The data is organized as an index with alphabetical links, so you must know what you're looking for before you begin. Otherwise, you will need to spend time scrolling through the links and site descriptions.

- There is no search engine provided. This is, however, the only drawback to using the site. The collection of links in the Data Finder includes everything from stock tracking and trading services to Federal Reserve Bank sites.
- From the Financial Data Finder, you can also click on links to the OSU Virtual Finance Library, which includes some excellent business resource tools, and the Business Job Finder, an online version of a good university career counseling center.

Other Sites

Economic Analysis Systems

http://www.econ-line.com/index.html

- U.S. Government economic data posted in spreadsheet format and available to download to your computer. Also includes links to other economic and financial research sites.

FinWeb

http://www.finweb.com

- Site maintained by James R. Garven, Ph.D., includes links to more academically oriented economics and finance journals, working papers, and databases. In addition, links to other finance and economics Web sites are available. A search engine increases the value of this directory.

U.S. Census Bureau

http://www.census.gov

- Official statistics from the U.S. Census Bureau, complete with tools that enable you to create your own extract files from the 1990 census data. Don't miss the Map Stats tool, which provides map profiles of cities and counties from across the country.

Cyber Atlas

http://www.cyberatlas.com

- Excellent tool for demographic and marketing information concerning the Internet and World Wide Web. Search statistical data that includes number of people on the Net, Web usage patterns, and breakdown of Web users by age, gender, and geographic location. Also includes articles, columns, and links to other Web marketing sites.

Get the Best Interest Rates

◆ **Bank Rate Monitor** ◆ **GetSmart** ◆ **FinanCenter**

Find the best interest rates for bank cards, real estate, and vehicle purchases. These sites supply financial calculators that you can use to weigh investment options. You can also apply for loans, mortgages, and credit cards at these sites.

Bank Rate Monitor

http://www.bankrate.com

 Find the latest interest rates for mortgages, car loans, credit cards, and other banking services.

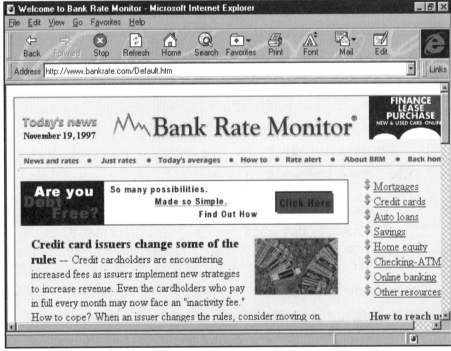

- Want to find the best interest rate for a company credit card? What about mortgage and other loan interest rates? If you need to find this information fast, Bank Rate Monitor should be the first place you check.

- Go to the Bank Rate Monitor home page, then click one of the links at the right of the page to find out the best available interest rates. Links include Mortgages, Credit cards, Auto loans, Checking-ATM, and Online banking.

- Click Mortgages to see mortgage trend information and links to rates in your area, state and national averages, loan cost comparison charts, and a simple mortgage calculator.

- The Credit cards page includes links you can use to search for the best available credit card deal. Also included are links you can use to search for gold cards, rebates, and cards that give you frequent flyer miles.

- The Online banking link takes you to a list of banks that offer special deals to Internet customers as well as a step-by-step guide to online banking.

- One of the top tools at this site is the Rate alert service. Click on the Rate alert link from the Bank Rate Monitor home page, then submit a form to indicate the type of rates you are interested in tracking. Bank Rate Monitor will send you e-mail to alert you when mortgage interest rates move up or down a tenth of a point or more. You can also follow changes in CD rates and in the Federal Reserve Bank's discount rate.

GetSmart

http://www.getsmart.com

 Find the best mortgage and credit card rates around. This site supplies the best search tools available for mortgage and credit card rates.

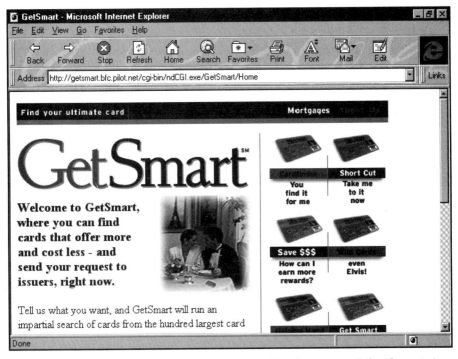

- Simplicity and focus count for a lot, and in the case of GetSmart, it pays off. Because GetSmart is focused only on credit cards and mortgages, it's an easy-to-use and very effective site. This is the best site on the Web for finding the right credit card and the best mortgage for you (not necessarily the one with the lowest rate).

- When the GetSmart home page opens, click either the Credit Card or the Mortgage button.

- If you click Credit Card, you see a list of search options at the right of the page. Each of these options cleverly anticipates the various ways in which you might want to look for a new card and explains the tool with a short, clear description. For example, click on Cardfinder if this fits what you want the search tool to do: "I tell you what I want. You find it for me." Click on Short Cut if you want the tool to do this: "I know the card I want. Take me to it now."

146

- Other credit card tools include Save$$$ ("How can I lower my payments? How can I earn more rewards?"), Helping Hand ("I'm having trouble getting credit. Help me get approved."), Get Smart ("I need the lowdown on credit cards. Give it to me straight."), and even a search tool called Wild Cards ("Cards for every personality… even Elvis.").

- Each of these search tools does a good job of asking the right questions to help you find the right card for your needs. For example, click Save$$$ and then decide whether you want to decrease your payments or earn more rewards (or both). Then enter the information and have the tools calculate how much more you can save or earn. After viewing the results, enter your Zip Code and click to see a list of recommended cards. You can then apply for a card online.

- The GetSmart Mortgage page is just as easy to use. Click on the Mortgage page, then select from any of the following options: I Want to Refinance My Home Loan, I've Found the Home, or I'm Just Shopping for a Home.

- Whichever option you click, you'll be asked to select the loan features that are important to you. You then figure out how much home you can afford and select a type of loan. Finally, you can choose the lender you want and start the approval process. With GetSmart, it's all very simple and easy to use.

- The GetSmart Mutual Funds page offers online financial advice on which mutual funds are best for you. GetSmart has access to all the 8,000+ mutual funds. A comparison chart outlines the unique services available to you. The cost of this service is a set-up fee and 1% per year on assets under management.

FinanCenter

http://www.financenter.com

This site bills itself as "Smart Personal Finance Made Easy," and it lives up to the promise by providing dozens of tools to help you weigh finance options.

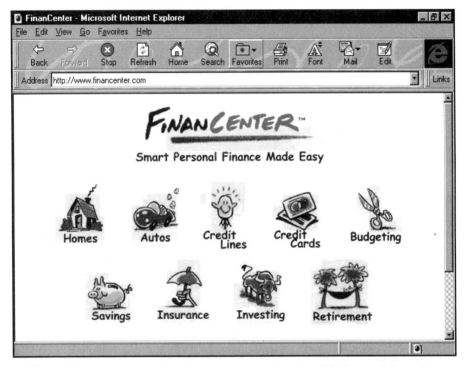

- FinanCenter appeals to the same urge to simplify financial matters as GetSmart. FinanCenter, however, includes a few more options besides home mortgages, credit cards, and mutual funds. This is more of a personal financial planning site. You can shop for car loans, insurance, credit lines, and plan for retirement, budgeting, and investing.

- Click on any of the tool icons to access a number of handy calculators. For example, the calculators on the Homes page include "How much can I borrow?," "How much will my payments be?," "Which is better: fixed or adjustable?," and "Am I better off renting?" Though these tools are geared for home ownership, the calculations can help you make business realty decisions as well. You can also click to find a realtor and see lenders' rates.

Research Investments

◆ The Street ◆ Morningstar ◆ Zacks
◆ CDA Investnet Insider Watch ◆ Other Sites

Use online investment research and analysis sites to make the best investment decisions for your portfolio. These sites offer market news, expert trader insight, as well as stock and fund comparison and screening tools. Sites include free research services as well as top-flight portfolio management for subscribers.

The Street

http://www.thestreet.com

Irreverent market commentary and analysis from a staff of Wall Street veterans with unfailing objectivity.

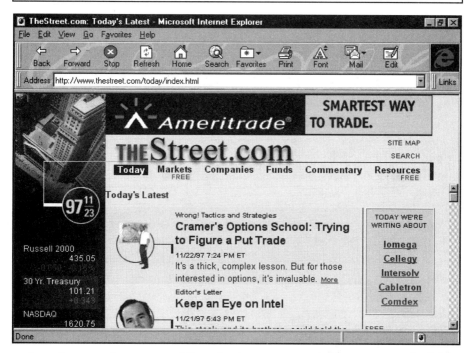

- Imagine you have round-the-clock access to the investment insight of a staff of top market analysts. Imagine that it costs you only about $7.00 a month. Now stop imagining and click on The Street.

- The Street offers the analysis of leading Wall Street columnists and editors such as James J. Cramer, a hedge fund manager and a founder of SmartMoney magazine. A hallmark of The Street is the combination of insider expertise and analysis with strict disclosure and objectivity standards—no staff reporters or editors can own stocks or positions except for mutual funds.

- In addition to market news and analysis, The Street offers an opinionated early morning e-mail round up of company news, market developments, mutual fund coverage, and analyst columns called Daily Bulletin.

- If you don't want the full range of Street services, you can still log on to The Street for free to get daily market news and access some services such as Lipper Analyticals Fund Facts and Scoreboards.

Morningstar

http://www.morningstar.net

 Get the low-down on mutual fund and stock market investing from the leading mutual fund investment firm and its database of more than 6,500 funds and more than 8,000 stocks.

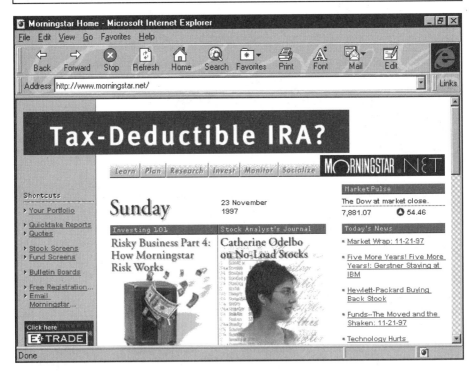

- Morningstar has made its name as the top provider of mutual fund data and analysis. Now you can have free access to a wealth of Morningstar investment research tools at the Morningstar site.

- The real gem here is the Data Screen tool. From the Morningstar home page, click on the Stock Screens or Fund Screens shortcut link. Next, select a stock sector or fund category from the lists provided, then select a screen. For example, you might want to find the ten best 3-year annualized returns for hybrid funds. Simply select those screening criteria and click to view the search results.

- Use the Monitor feature to check fund winners and losers on the current day's trading. Click the Plan page to review articles and features on preparing your investment strategy. You can also monitor up to ten portfolios using the Morningstar site.

- This complete investing tool also includes a Learn page with links to news, articles, and expert advice on building and managing your own portfolio. Click on articles including Investing 101: Funds, Investing 101: Stocks, or The Guestroom, where featured columnists hold forth.

Zacks

http://www.zacks.com

 Harness the power of the leading institutional investor research service.

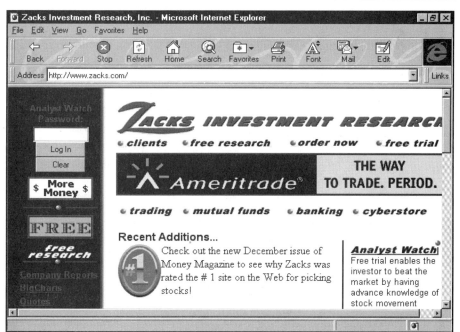

- Here's a powerful fact to consider: The Zacks Recommended 100 stock universe, since its inception on February 12, 1996, has shown a return of 65.5% through November 7, 1997, compared to the S&P 500 return of 36.2% during the same time period.
- Zacks is a full-service market analysis service used by institutional money managers, but if you're serious about the success of your investment portfolio, the wide range of subscription services, including the Zacks 100, may be well worth the money.
- Even if you don't want to pay for the many Zacks' fee-based services, there are of free investment research services available at the Zacks site, including charting software, brokerage research, historical financial tables, and earnings surprises.
- This is an investment research site where the subscription services are top of the line and the free tools go far beyond what many other services offer.

CDA Investnet Insider Watch

http://www.cda.com/investnet/

 Leading site for insider trading alerts and analysis. Get the inside scoop on Wall Street stock movement.

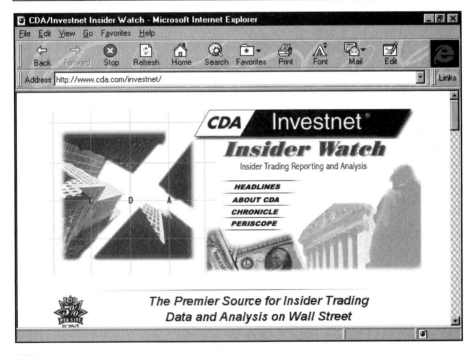

- Who knows more about the financial and business outlook of a company than its senior management? What better source than senior management trading of company stock to gauge your own investment activity? CDA Investnet Insider Watch is the Web's leading site for insider trading alerts and analysis.
- Access this free site for insider trading tips, alerts, and watches. Another great tool is the insider trading spotlight table, listing the biggest insider trades. The table includes company name, insider name and title, dollar and share amount of trade, and transaction dates.
- You can also download a free issue of the CDA Insider Chronicle newsletter. Viewing the newsletter requires an Adobe Acrobat file viewer such as Acrobat Reader or Acrobat Exchange. A trial subscription for the weekly newsletter is also available.
- Perhaps the best free tool available at the CDA site is the link to Periscope, a weekly insider-trading column that delivers excellent detailed insider trading analysis.

Other Sites

INVESTools

http://www.investools.com

- Top-notch investment research advice for independent investors. Complete suite of research tools and links to third party sites.

IPO Central

http://www.ipocentral.com

- Leading source for IPO (initial public offering) filing information. Free access to listings of the most recent IPO filings and company filing data.

Silicon Investor

http://www.techstocks.com

- Individual investor site that emphasizes interactivity and investor chat through its StockTalk feature.

FreeEDGAR

http://www.freeedgar.com

- Get real-time access to SEC filings free of charge. Access vital company information and estimate the intrinsic value of companies using the discounted cash flow calculator.

Find Professional Services and Suppliers

◆ **LocalEyes** ◆ **IOMA Business Directory** ◆ **BigBook** ◆ **Other Sites**

Search for professional services, suppliers, and other businesses on the Web. Find potential customers and clients with these leading directories.

LocalEyes

http://www8.localeyes.com

 Find business and professional services in dozens of metro areas across the country with this "yellow pages" type directory and search tool.

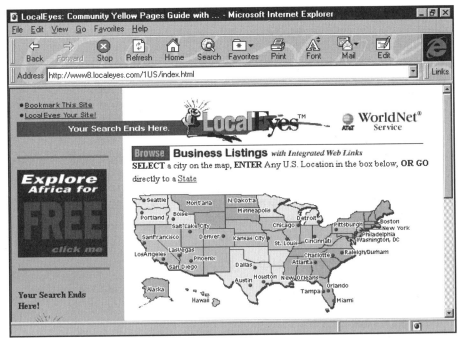

- Use the LocalEyes search site to find business resources in your community or any area across the country. From the LocalEyes home page you can enter a search phrase such as Accountants in Cleveland, then click Search. From the search results, you can then click a link and go directly to the firm or site you want.

154

- From the home page, you can also enter a city, state, or Zip Code for a list of LocalEyes regions. Click a region link to go to a LocalEyes metro page. From a metro page you can select a directory category such as Business & Professional or Money & Finance to narrow your search.

- You can also enter a business name or topic in the search engine at a metro page to search LocalEyes listings only in that area. Include a Zip Code in the search criteria to narrow the search further.

- LocalEyes also includes links to other metro area sites such as shopping mall listings, weather, TV listings, and recommended Great Sites.

IOMA Business Directory
http://www.ioma.com/directory

 IOMA Web site directory includes dozens of links to business resources.

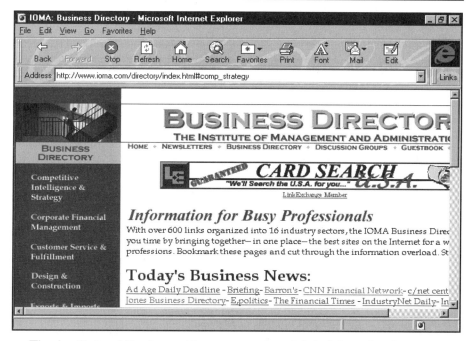

- The Institute of Business Management and Administration is a valuable Web site simply for its Business Directory. The site also features dozens of newsletters and management discussion groups.

- The directory is broken down into several category links, including Corporate Financial Management, Information Systems, Insurance & Risk, Manufacturing, Public Accounting, Small Business, and Web Site Management.

- Click one of these categories to see a listing of related links. Most categories present several dozen links to other business sites on the Web. There is no further organization or explanation of the sites, but the purpose of most is self-explanatory.

- If you click the Corporate Financial Management link in the left column, you'll get the Corporate Financial Management links page. Links on that page include: Attorney's National, Dun and Bradstreet Online Solutions, Audit Center, Institute of Internal Auditors, Trade Point USA, etc.

- The value of having many outstanding business resource links such as these collected at one directory makes this a can't-miss site.

BigBook

http://www.bigbook.com

 Find any business or professional service quickly. Listings include exact location shown on a map as well as driving directions.

- BigBook is one of the leading online yellow pages sites, offering numerous added value services that can help you find the business or professional service firm you're looking for quickly and easily.

156

(e.g. Hotels) in the search text box and then enter a city and/or state to search. You can also click on links to available search categories.

- If you want to find nearby businesses, you can use either the Search Nearby tool or the Detailed Search tool. With Search Nearby, you can specify a business or category and then a distance from a specific address. For example, I found that there are 30 lawyers and 8 pizza parlors within a 1-mile radius of my home address.

- With Detailed Search, you can specify a business or category and then a specific street name, area code, city, state, or Zip Code to search. The search results will list all of the businesses you asked for in that specific location. For example, there are 40 CPAs listed in the 46220 Zip Code in Indianapolis.

- After you receive the search results page, which includes addresses and phone numbers, you can click on a specific listing to see a map showing the business location. Click on the Driving Directions icon and enter your location to find out how to get there.

- BigBook also includes links to sales leads, mailing lists, business profiles, and credit ratings provided by American Business Information.

Other Sites

Four11

http://www.four11.com

- Find someone's e-mail address or phone number with this site. Four11 also includes a yellow pages business listing and a listing of 800 numbers.

Switchboard

http://www.switchboard.com

- Find people or businesses with this directory site. The cool SideClick feature helps you surf the Web "sideways" to find Web sites related to ones you like.

Toll-Free Internet Directory

http://www.tollfree.att.net/dir800/

- Use this searchable directory to find toll-free phone numbers.

BigYellow

http://www.bigyellow.com

- This top-flight yellow pages directory includes more than 16 million U.S. business listings.

Research Companies

◆ **BRINT** ◆ **Hoover's Online** ◆ **Dun & Bradstreet**
◆ **Fuld Competitive Intelligence** ◆ **Other Sites**

Search online databases for company information to help you evaluate credit-worthiness of potential customers, research potential clients, and analyze competitors.

BRINT

http://www.brint.com/interest.html

Excellent search and directory site for finding corporate and competitive information. Hundreds of links to important business Web resources.

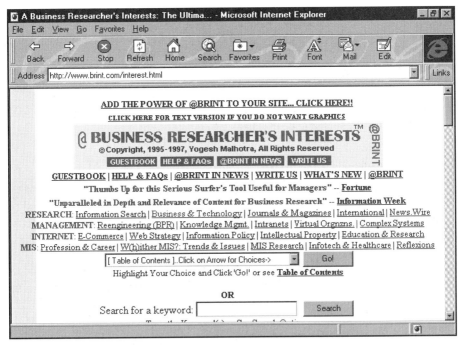

- In many cases, the top Web sites to know are those that can lead you to many other sites. These sites are useful time and again even as your search needs change. The Business Researcher's Interests site (BRINT) is one of the top directory sites for sales research on the Net.

158

- To find corporate and competitive information, click the Business and Technology link and then click the Company and Industry Information link. From here, you can click on a number of specific Web site links to search for the competitive information you need.

- Company and Industry Information links include more than three dozen top business search sites, such as the Forbes 500 Annual Directory, and Marketing: The Biggest and Best.

- From these Web directories you can find specific company information.

Hoover's Online
http://www.hoovers.com

 Search for free company information at the Hoover's Web site. Hoover's online bills itself as "the ultimate source for company information."

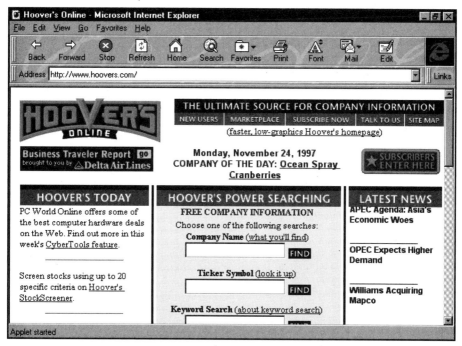

- Hoover's, Inc., is one of the leading publishers of company information, and its Web site is perhaps the best source for low-cost (and free) company data. Hoover's is well known as a publisher of company capsules on more than 11,000 public and private companies around the world.

- Through the Hoover's Web site you can search for a capsule by name or ticker symbol, sort companies based on industry, location, and/or sales. Each company capsule contains basic information you can use to locate, communicate with, and analyze a company.

- To search the Hoover's list of company capsules, go to the home page and enter the company name, a stock ticker symbol, or a keyword. You can also see a business news ticker on the home page.

- Click the Research Stocks link to go to a full-feature investor research page. Click the Boost Your Sales link to see a page that has sales resources such as articles, tips, and links to top sales Web sites.

- Another feature on the Hoover's site you don't want to miss is the Hoover's List of Lists. This page lists links to sites that rank businesses and people in many different categories, including The Biggest & Richest Companies & People, Top Brands, Top Salaries, and Stock Market Performance. Go to: http://hoovers.com/features/whosontop/lists.html.

- Other Hoover's Web sites include IPO Central, Cyberstocks, and Stock Screener. Links to each of these sites can be found on the Hoover's Online site.

Dun & Bradstreet

http://www.dnb.com

 Search the Companies Online database of Dun & Bradstreet, the world's leading distributor of company business and financial information and credit reporting.

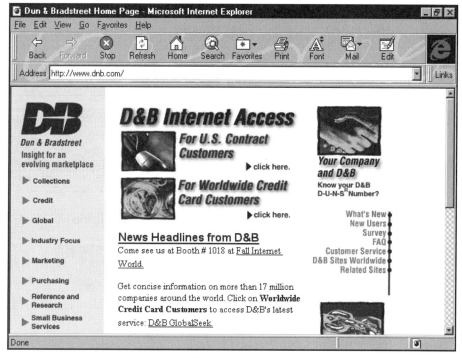

- Log on to the Dun & Bradstreet site primarily to search the Companies Online database, which has been created in partnership with Lycos. You can enter a company name, ticker symbol, and/or URL to begin your free search.

- If you turn up results, you will see a general listing for the company, which includes basic contact information and ownership structure. If you register (free of charge), you can receive information on number of employees, annual sales, holding companies, and other more in-depth data.

- For a $20 fee you can order the Dun & Bradstreet Business Background Report for the company.

- Though Dun & Bradstreet provides excellent, detailed company intelligence, credit reports, and other consulting services, you won't find much more that's free on the Web site. Most links are to marketing or catalog information on Dun & Bradstreet subscriber products.

Fuld Competitive Intelligence

http://www.fuld.com

Fuld & Company corporate site provides numerous links to Web company information resources.

- The Fuld & Company corporate Web site is a great place to start your search for information about competitors and corporate customers. Though this is primarily a corporate marketing site for Fuld's consulting services, you can click the Internet Intelligence Index icon to see a list of links to competitive intelligence sites.

- Links are organized into three general categories: General Business Internet Resources, Industry-Specific Internet Resources, and International Internet Resources.

- General Business Resources links of interest in researching competitors and customers include Company Information, Competitor Intelligence Sites, and Information Services. Click one of these to see links to specific company information sites.

- Industry-Specific Resources links include nearly two dozen industry category links, from Aerospace/Defense to Travel. Click on the industry link you want to search to see links to specific sites. For example, click on the Retailing link to access links to the National Retailing Federation and The World Wide Web Virtual Library for Retailing.

Other Sites

Infoseek Business Channel

http://www.infoseek.com

- Click on the Business channel of this search and directory site to find a wealth of top business links and access to the Hoover's Online company capsules.

Lycos Companies Online

http://www.lycos.com

- Lycos Business Guide includes many valuable business links, Lycos' famous Top 5% sites, and the ability to search the Companies Online database of corporate information, which Lycos runs in partnership with Dun & Bradstreet.

Find Real Estate

◆ Net Properties ◆ ICSC Shopping Center Database
◆ National Real Estate Investor ◆ Homebuyer's Fair ◆ Other Sites

Use these top sites to find commercial or residential real estate and research relocation options. There are dozens of very good real estate search sites on the Web. These sites offer special tools and exceptional search capabilities to help you make the right choices when buying or leasing property.

Net Properties

http://www.netprop.com

 Search for commercial or residential real estate on twin sites called Homenet and Centernet.

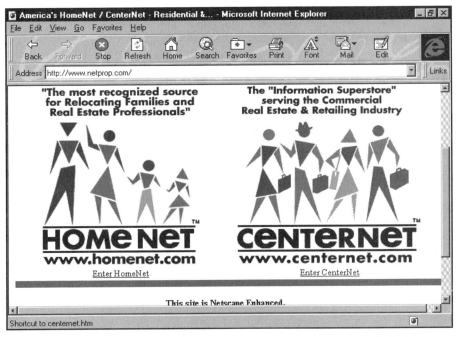

- The Net Properties Web site offers links to what are essentially two separate sites: Homenet for residential real estate and Centernet for commercial real estate.

164

- From the Net Properties home page, click on Centernet to use its searchable database of commercial properties available for sale or lease nationwide. At the Centernet home page, click on the Property Database link to start using the search engine. Click one of the two globe icons to select properties for lease or for sale.

- You can enter a number of search criteria at the Properties for Sale and Properties for Lease pages, including property type, year built range, minimum and maximum prices, minimum and maximum square feet, and location. You can then click on property listings from the search results page.

- Other resources available at the Centernet site include links to news, real estate companies, products and services, trade journals, and associations. You can also list your company at Centernet.

- From the Net Properties home page, click on Homenet to search residential listings nationwide. At the Homenet home page, click on the U.S. Real Estate Directory link to start your search, then click on a state to narrow the search location.

- Once you get to the Real Estate directory page of the state you choose, your best bet is to click the Real Estate Company Directory to see a listing of links by county to real estate agency sites. From here you can search the agency sites for many more listings than you will find on the Homenet properties residential database.

- Also available on the Homenet site are links to various services such as census data, a mortgage calculator, and lenders.

ICSC Shopping Center Database

http://www.icsc.org/le/database.html

 Search the ICSC database for commercial real estate leasing and purchase opportunities.

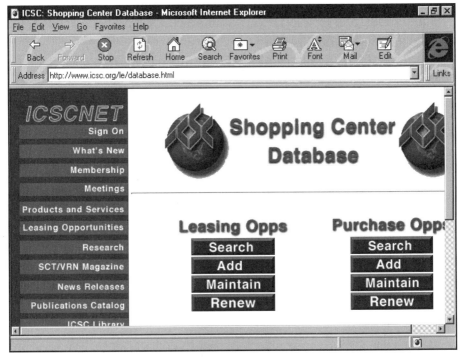

- The International Council of Shopping Centers (ICSC) is the not-for-profit trade association of the shopping center industry. The ICSC Web site offers a wide range of industry information and resources, but the primary attraction is the searchable database of commercial real estate.

- Click Search in either the Leasing Opportunities or Purchase Opportunities categories. Searching for lease opportunities will lead to more search results because the purchase category only lists entire shopping centers that are for sale.

- Enter your search criteria into the Leasing Opportunities form and click for results. Search criteria can include available square feet, location, center type, center features, and available space features.

- You can also add, maintain, and renew real estate listings in the ICSC database from this Web site. You can search and add listings to the database even if you are not a member of the association.

National Real Estate Investor

http://www.internetreview.com/pubs/nrei/nrei.htm

 Keep up-to-date on commercial real estate with the online version of this leading investor magazine.

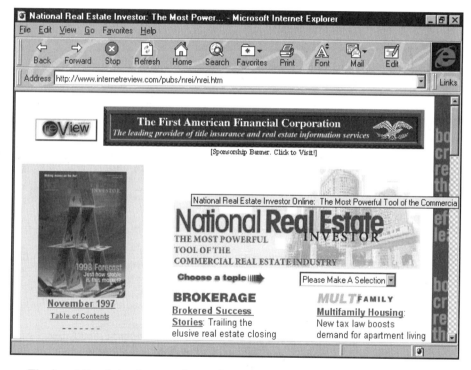

- Find out the latest news from the world of commercial real estate with National Real Estate Investor magazine's online version. This publication is widely regarded as the leading source for real estate transaction and industry news.

- Check for articles by category, then click to read the full text. More than a dozen search categories are available, including Brokerage, City/Area Reviews, Company Profiles, Corporate Real Estate, Financing, Office, Real Estate Services, and Retail. All searches show results from back issues as well as current ones.

- This site does not include any real estate search tools, but the timely information on the commercial real estate market is worth a look if you are considering an investment or just looking for more space.
- Click on the reView icon at the top of the page to go to the Internet Review Online home page. Internet Review Online serves the commercial real estate industry with information databases and several publications whose Web sites you can access from the reView home page.

Homebuyer's Fair

http://www.homefair.com/home/

 Use this site to make informed decisions about relocating employees or making a move yourself.

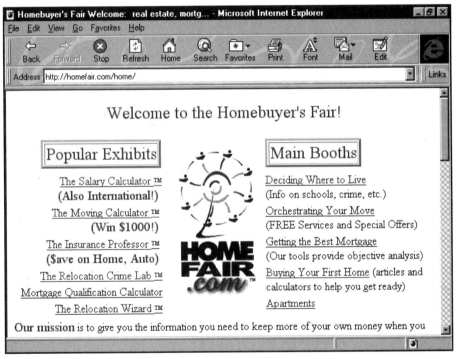

- Use Homebuyer's Fair to consider all the angles when you make your next move. This popular site includes a number of interactive tools to help you decide where you want to buy and how best to do it.

- The most useful tool at this site when considering a possible transfer is the Salary Calculator. Use the calculator to see how much you have to make in a new city to match your current salary. The results can be surprising—this is a good check to use before you leap at the opportunity to go somewhere new.

- Try the Relocation Crime Lab to compare crime rates between cities. This is an interesting tool to look up the number of crimes in your city even if you're not considering a move.

- Use the Relocation Wizard to create a customized timeline of tasks for making a smooth move. The resulting to-do list can be a handy, if somewhat daunting, reminder of all there is to do before the big day.

- All of the tools in Homebuyer's Fair are very interactive and fun to use. You'll find this site to be an invaluable resource for your next move.

Other Sites

HomeScout

http://www.homescout.com

- Excellent search engine for hundreds of residential Web sites. Search more than 500,000 listings.

HomeBuyer

http://www.homebuyer.com

- Rated as a NetGuide Gold site, this full-service residential real estate site includes a complete directory of Buyer's Agents.

International Real Estate Digest

http://www.ired.com

- Complete site of real estate search and information links catering to real estate professionals. Powerful search tools and more than 1000 pages of searchable articles.

MoveQuest

http://www.movequest.com

- Step-by-step how-to site walks you through the entire relocation process, from finding the right home to getting settled in to your new neighborhood.

Hire Employees or Find a Job

◆ **The Monster Board** ◆ **Virtual Job Fair**
◆ **America's Job Bank** ◆ **Other Sites**

Avoid the high cost of hiring with recruiters by checking these Web sites. Most of these sites offer databases of resumes submitted by those seeking jobs. You can search these databases after registering with the site and/or paying a small fee. If you're looking for a career change, you can search the extensive databases of job openings at these sites free of charge. Also check into career planning resources and links to employer Web pages available at most of these sites.

The Monster Board

http://www.monsterboard.com

 Premier full-service job search and recruitment Web site offers career development and search agent services.

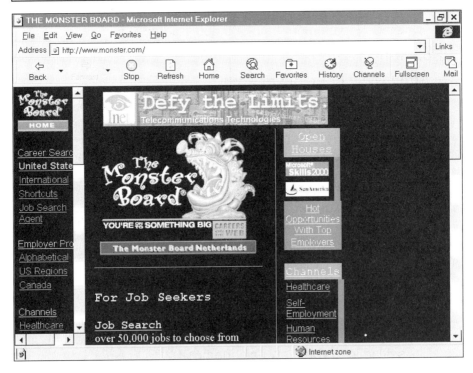

- Use The Monster Board to find your next star employee or find the next spot on your hike up the career ladder.

- Click the Career Search link to start looking for a job. On the Career Search Welcome page you can choose either a U.S. or International search of more than 8,500 total employers. Click the Personal Job Search Agent link to launch Swoop, a character in keeping with the monster site theme, who will zero in on job listings that fit a personal search profile you create.

- You can also click on Shortcut job search links such as healthcare, human resources, entry level, internship opportunities, and outdoor work.

- Click the Employer Profiles link to see an index of online company information brochures.

- Click the Career Center link to use the resume builder tool, check listings of upcoming hiring events, browse articles, get career advice, and check apartment and relocation listings.

- If you're looking for employees, click the Recruiters Center link. At the Recruiters Center you can search the Monster database of more than 200,000 resumes, use a resume search agent called 'Cruiter, or post a job on the site.

Virtual Job Fair

http://www.vjf.com/pub/jobsearch.html

Top site for finding a job or hiring employees in the high-tech industries.

- Westech's Virtual Job Fair is designed to serve job seekers and employers in high-tech industries. Technical professionals will find that the Westech service yields superior results because it is targeted to high-tech companies.

- Westech sponsors ongoing job fairs in cities across the country and provides information about upcoming fairs at the Web site.

- Westech also publishes High Technology Careers Magazine, which you can access online by clicking the High Tech Careers icon. Here you can browse magazine articles and columns as well as search the alphabetical Employer's Directory.

- Click on the Job Search icon to enter search criteria for the Westech high-tech job database. This is a high-traffic site and should yield good results if you're looking for a high-tech job—more than 250,000 job search queries are processed by the Web site each day.

172

- Go to the Resume Center to submit your resume to the Virtual Job Fair. You can post resumes either in a public or private area of the site. Employers must register to search the resume database.

America's Job Bank

http://www.ajb.dni.us/index.html

 Post job openings free of charge on this site produced by a network of state employment agencies. Easy-to-use job search tools make this site well worthwhile.

- Now you can put all of those unemployment insurance tax dollars to work for you by using the America's Job Bank Web site. This site is produced by the public Employment Service, a network of state employment agencies across the country.

- While not quite as feature-rich as other job search Web sites, all the basics are here, and employers can post job openings on the site free of charge. The site is funded by state unemployment insurance taxes.

- To post a job, click on the Employers link at the home page. You must fill out a brief registration form to use the employers service, but after doing so you can post jobs, link your Web site to the America's Job Bank site, use recruiting services, and use an automatic job posting service.

- If you're looking for a job, click on the Job Seekers link from the home page. The search tools at this site are easy to use and you can search using either a drop-down list of occupations and locations, a keyword search, or federal and military job codes. Click on the Employers Sites link to see an alphabetical index of more than 2,000 company Web pages.

- Click on the Job Market Info link to see career development information, including geographic profiles of state demographics, job search resources, and an interesting list of career trends showing what jobs and fields are expected to grow in the next ten years.

Other Sites

CareerPath.com

http://career.careerpath.com

- Founded and backed by six major newspapers, this site offers job hunters more than 150,000 positions no older than two weeks, gathered from employers' Web sites and the want ads of 45 newspapers across the country.

Online Career Center

http://www.occ.com

- This award-winning site was the first job clearinghouse page on the Web. Excellent career resources and easy-to-use job database searching make this site worth visiting.

E-Span

http://www.espan.com

- This site provides more in-depth screening services for both employers and job seekers to ensure that the right person is matched to the right job. There are fewer job listings here than at other sites, but greater selectivity in the screening process means a better chance of finding what you want.

Find Small Business Resources

◆ smallbizNet ◆ Idea Cafe ◆ Small Business Administration
◆ Trade-direct ◆ Other Sites

Use the sites listed here to help you run your small business. These sites offer free resources, support, services, and information that can make the busy life of an entrepreneur much easier.

smallbizNet

http://www.lowe.org/smbiznet/index.htm

Search this online small business resource database and directory of business links. Access interactive business tools at the Edge Online magazine.

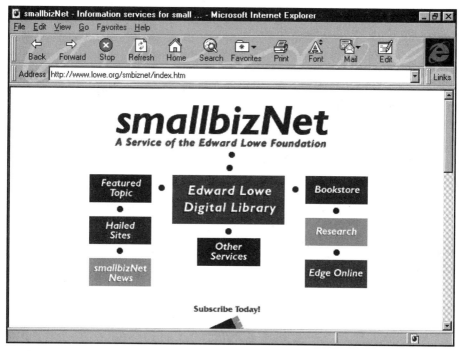

- Consult the smallbizNet site to find small business resources and information. The site is provided by the Edward Lowe Foundation, which is dedicated to helping small business owners and entrepreneurs succeed.

- Click on Hailed Sites to access a directory of nearly 200 links to business Web sites. A subject index of links to the sites contains 48 categories to aid you in your search. Categories range from Accounting to Franchising to Women and Small Business.

- Click on the Edward Lowe Digital Library to search 4,000 indexed and abstracted documents pertaining to small business management. Documents have been culled from books, government agencies, and online publishers.

- Click the Edge Online link to go to the Lowe Foundation's other Web site, a digital version of Entrepreneurial Edge magazine. Edge Online includes interactive financial and business management tools at its Business Builders and Interactive Toolbox links that can provide even a large, well-established firm with useful resources.

Idea Cafe

http://www.ideacafe.com

 Check the Idea Cafe for a look at the "soft skills" side of small business ownership. Provides a boost to your creative and competitive spirit.

- The Idea Cafe is a Web site devoted to keeping small business ownership fun. The site has a light tone that focuses on the "soft skills" side of business—keeping your mental attitude on an even keel and dealing with the stress of running a business on your own.

- Aside from a somewhat distracting color scheme and graphics on the Web site, the content here is a nice change of pace from the more bottom-line oriented business sites that abound on the Web.

- There are few business tools available on the site. Instead, you will find articles offering advice on how to keep the mental edge you need to be successful. This site is definitely worth checking when you're feeling a little overwhelmed by work and need a boost.

Small Business Administration

http://www.sbaonline.sba.gov/

 Rich and authoritative site for free small business resources, courtesy of the federal government.

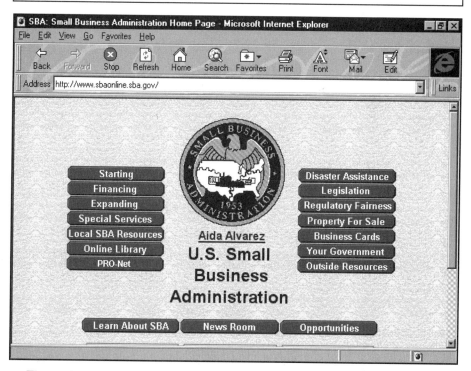

- The U.S. government's Small Business Administration (SBA) Web site is the authoritative source for information about small business regulation and government resources. The site contains resources that you can't find elsewhere.

- Click on the Starting link to find resources such as sample business plans, links to more than 500 shareware programs, special assistance and counseling, and patent and trademark information.

- You can also find links to local SBA resources, property for sale, financing sources, and a link to SBA's PRO-Net, a database of procurement information for small businesses.

- Unlike many offline government services, the SBA Web site is well-organized and easy to use. You only need to click once or twice to access useful tools and services.

Trade-direct

http://www.trade-direct.com

 Buy and sell with confidence over the Web using this low-cost facilitator site.

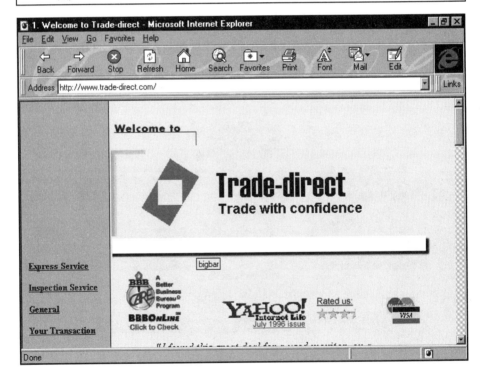

- This unique online service facilitates buying and selling between two parties who have found each other over the Internet. Buyer pays Trade-direct the agreed-to purchase amount plus a small additional fee. The seller ships the item to the buyer, and Trade-direct holds the money until the buyer confirms that he is satisfied with the purchase.

- If the buyer is satisfied, Trade-direct sends the money minus its fee to the seller. If the buyer is not satisfied, he can return the merchandise and Trade-direct returns all money it received. You can take advantage of this service through the Trade-direct Express Service link.

- For transactions larger than $3,000, you can use the Trade-direct Inspection Service, in which goods are shipped to Trade-direct for its inspection before the money changes hands.

- This service is an ingenious way to help buyers and sellers conduct risk-free business transactions online.

Other Sites

Lycos Small Business Resource Guide

http://www.lycos.com/resources/smallbiz/index.html

- The site Provides as extensive directory of links to small business resources from one of the Web's leading search tools.

Better Business Bureau

http://www.bbb.org/

- Use the Bureau's business report database to see alerts about fraudulent business practices. Join the Bureau and use online dispute resolution.

Use Reference Tools

◆ Elements of Style ◆ Library of Congress
◆ Learn2 ◆ Other Sites

Need to find an answer fast? Use these sites to track down that elusive piece of information.

Elements of Style

http://www.columbia.edu/acis/bartleby/strunk/

 Find the best way to get your point across by referring to this classic reference work for written communication.

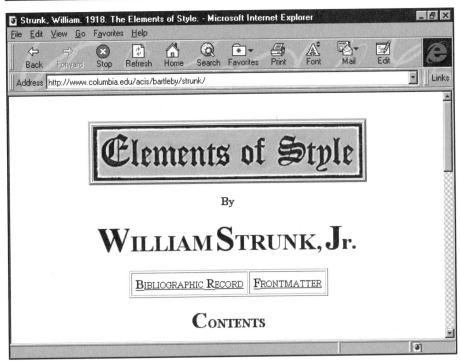

- If you need to find the best way to express your thoughts, refer to The Elements of Style's simple rules for writing clearly. Bookmark this Web page for ready access to this classic style guide.

- From the Elements of Style contents page you can click on links to any chapter of the book you care to read. The complete text of the work is available.

- The site is provided by the Project Bartleby online library of literary, historical, and reference works, created by Columbia University. Project Bartleby was the first to publish a book on the Web (Whitman's Leaves of Grass) in February 1994. The New Bartleby Library is now an independent entity from Columbia University.

Library of Congress

http://ftp.loc.gov/

 Search the holdings and major exhibitions of our nation's largest repository of information.

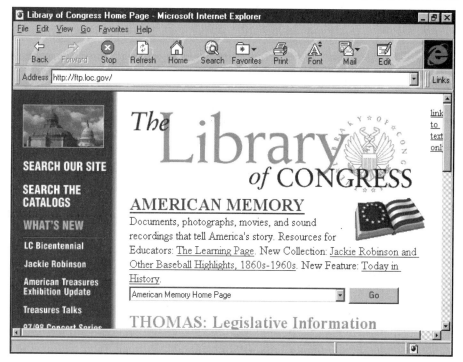

- Though not the easiest Web site to use, it's all here—the complete contents of the Library of Congress in searchable database form.

- You can search either the LOC Web site or the library's catalog of holdings. The Web site search is still under development and contains an alphabetical index of the links within the LOC site.

- Click Search the Catalogs to begin browsing the LOC catalogs. You can use either a word search or a browse search. Some of the records found by the word search contain links to digitized materials available online. Browse search results yield only the LOC catalog information for materials.

- Perhaps the most appealing part of this site is access to text and images from the library's ongoing exhibitions, the THOMAS database of information about the activities of the U.S. Congress, and the Learning Page for K-12 grade students. Another interesting link is the LOC's Today in History feature.

Learn2

http://www.learn2.com

 Find out how to do thousands of common and practical tasks by reading Learn2 tutorials.

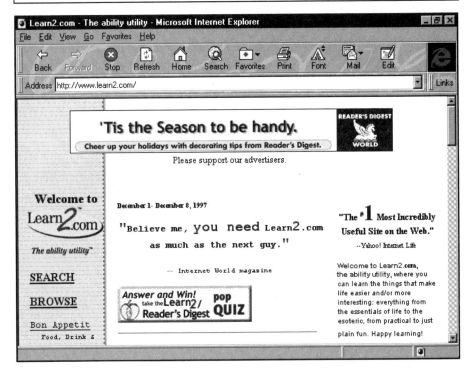

- Learn2.com bills itself as "the ability utility." This is a Web site where you can learn how to do a thousand and one very practical tasks.

- Use the search engine to find what you want to do or click one of the category links.
- Learn2 tutorials are quick, concise, and easy to understand. Ever wonder how to increase your fuel mileage? A three-part tutorial on how to do just that was recently featured at the Learn2 home page. In ten minutes you can learn how to save a few dollars a week—which can really add up.
- Category links include everything from Bon Apetit for food, drink, and entertaining to Your Turn, tutorials (or 2torials in the lingo of the Learn2 page) about sports, games, and recreation.
- If you don't find what you're looking for through the category links, type your topic in the search engine text box. This site is no substitute for formal training, but you can pick up some interesting nuggets of knowledge, detailed and practical how-to information that can help you save money or time.

Other Sites

Bartlett's Quotations

http://www.columbia.edu/acis/bartleby/bartlett/

- Another service of Columbia University's Project Bartleby, this site provides the entire text of Bartlett's Familiar Quotations complete with a search engine. You can also browse alphabetical and chronological indexes of links to author quotes.

Webster's Dictionary and Thesaurus

http://www.m-w.com/dictionary

- Look up words or phrases online with this Web version of the classic American dictionary. Also includes a thesaurus and such Word of the Day features as games, What's in a Name, Coined by Shakespeare, and Rappers to Flappers: American Youth Slang.

National Archives

http://www.nara.gov

- Entertaining and enlightening site includes hardcore reference links to government information such as the Federal Register and Code of Federal Regulations. Browse The Visitor's Gallery for online exhibitions and educational programs. The Research Room includes links to historical records useful in tracing people, places, and events.

Plan and Book Travel Online

◆ **Microsoft Expedia** ◆ **Bed and Breakfast Inns Online** ◆ **Zagat Survey**
◆ **MapQuest** ◆ **Other Sites**

Use the Web to make your next business trip more enjoyable and more cost effective. There are dozens of excellent travel-related sites that can help you plan your trip, search for travel bargains, and book tickets online. These top travel Web sites provide a good sample of the kinds of resources available online to help you.

Microsoft Expedia

http://expedia.msn.com/daily/home/default.hts

 Use this award-winning Web site to explore destinations, plan your trip itinerary, and book travel online.

- Microsoft Expedia is the award-winning travel Web site produced by the software giant as part of its Microsoft Network online service. The site has been named one of the top 100 Web sites by PC Magazine, a Yahoo! Internet Life Five-Star Award-winner (one of only 12 per year), and a Top Ten PCWeek E-Commerce winner.

- The site receives these awards with good reason. First, it's a pleasure to look at, with a rich attractive Web page design. It's also full of information about where to go and what to do. Click on the Resources link to browse the World Guide, a complete online travel guidebook, check weather, and use a currency converter.

- Click on Magazine to read articles about travel destinations, news briefs and bargain updates, as well as featured columnists and ideas about fresh approaches to travel that can make your trip more enjoyable.

- The beauty of most travel Web sites is the capability to plan and book travel online. Expedia offers a number of powerful search and booking tools at its Travel Agent link. Click here to find low airfares and book airline tickets. You can also search for available hotel rooms at your destination and reserve rooms. If you need a rental car, you can find and reserve one here too.

Bed and Breakfast Inns Online
http://www.bbonline.com

 Find a distinctive place to stay on your next business trip that will save you money and allow you to enjoy your destination more.

- One way to make business travel more enjoyable is to avoid cookie-cutter chain hotels and stay at a small inn that lets you experience a little more of what life is like in the town you're visiting.

- Bed & Breakfasts Online provides a guide to more than 2,000 bed and breakfasts and country inns across the United States. You may be surprised by how many fine inns are available at very reasonable rates, in many cases less expensive than staying at a chain hotel.

- You will also find that many inns and bed and breakfasts are located in major cities, close to where you do business. Click on the Locate a B&B link at the Bed & Breakfasts Online home page to begin your search.

- You can search the site's database by location in the United States, Canada, Mexico, and the Caribbean. U.S. listings are organized by region and then by state.

- You can also search several directories of inns with distinctive features, such as being on the ocean or in the mountains, being on the National Register of Historic Places, or those offering special package deals. The site also includes links to state innkeeper association Web sites.

Zagat Survey

http://www.pathfinder.com/travel/Zagat

Find the right restaurant for your next business meal by consulting the Zagat Survey online. Complete directory of survey listings and reviews for 40 major U.S. cities.

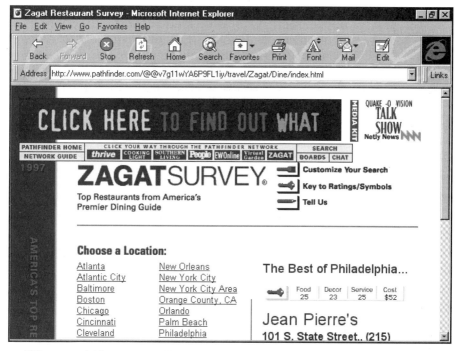

- What could be worse than dropping big bucks on a meal with a client (or prospective client) and having the meal turn out to be less than impressive, even downright awful? Consulting the Zagat Survey Web site beforehand is a great way to avoid a bad business meal on the road.

- The Zagat Survey is widely recognized as the leading guide to fine dining across the country. Click on a city link to view an alphabetical index of restaurant listings for the city. You can also search the listings directory by cuisine, by food ranking, or by best deals.

- If you already know the name of the restaurant you want to find, just type it into the search engine text box and click on Find It!

- Each link to a restaurant listing has a one- or two-word description of the type of restaurant (such as French, vegetarian, or Tex-Mex) to help you sift among the many possibilities. Click on a restaurant link to read the Zagat review. The survey rates each restaurant by food, decor, and service on a scale of 0 to 30. The cost of an average dinner plus drink and tip is also listed.

MapQuest

http://www.mapquest.com

 Don't get lost on your way to an important appointment. Check the MapQuest site for door-to-door driving directions and interactive maps of any location in the continental U.S.

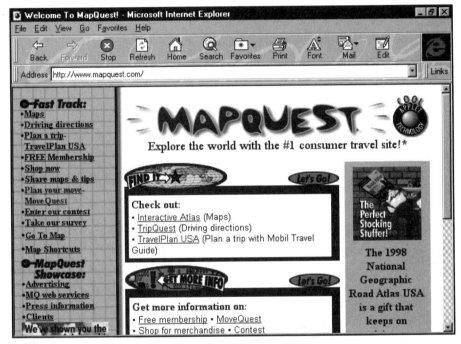

- Need to know how to get to your next appointment? Head for the MapQuest Web site to find out the best way to get to your destination.

- Click on the TripQuest link to find driving directions from point A to point B. Simply type the address of your starting point in the TripQuest form, then type in the address of your destination.

- You can choose several mapping options for your directions, including city-to-city or door-to-door with an overview map, turn-by-turn maps with text, or text only. Door-to-door directions are provided for 29 major metro areas. City-to-city routing is provided from any town or city to any other town or city within the continental U.S. and some parts of Mexico and Canada.

- If you want to find your own way, click on the Interactive Atlas link on the home page. At the Interactive Atlas page, you can enter a point of interest or an address to view a map of that location. You can zoom in or zoom out to view more or less area and detail on the maps.

- Click on the TravelPlan USA link at the MapQuest home page to plan your next trip using the Mobil Travel Guide.

Other Sites

The Trip
http://www.thetrip.com

- Among the many travel Web sites available, The Trip stands out because of its attention to the needs of business travelers. The Trip has a no-nonsense, no-hassle approach to planning and booking enjoyable travel. Be sure to check out the Airport Strategies link for information about making your flight connections.

FareFinder
http://www.reservations.com/Farefinder/

- To find the lowest airfares available today, check Preview Travel's Farefinder service. A ticker of lowest fares between various cities nationwide appears at the top of the page. Enter your departure city and destination to find the lowest fares currently available.

Subway Navigator
http://metro.jussieu.fr:10001/bin/cities/english

- Find the route from one destination to another using this routing service for subway or rail systems in major cities around the world.

Travlang Foreign Languages for Travelers
http://www.travlang.com

- Extensive directory of language resources for study and translation of languages from around the world. Includes links to Web resources for even the most obscure languages. The site also offers international travel services such as overseas hotel listings, air reservations, and currency exchange information.

Track Shipments

◆ UPS ◆ FedEx ◆ Other Sites

Track your business's shipments using shipping company Web sites. Both of the world's top package shipping companies, Federal Express and UPS, have very useful sites that can help you decide the most cost-effective way to send packages, track packages, and even prepare and print shipping forms using your computer and laser printer.

UPS

http://www.ups.com

 Complete shipping rate information and detailed drop-off site locator which includes site addresses, maps, and directions.

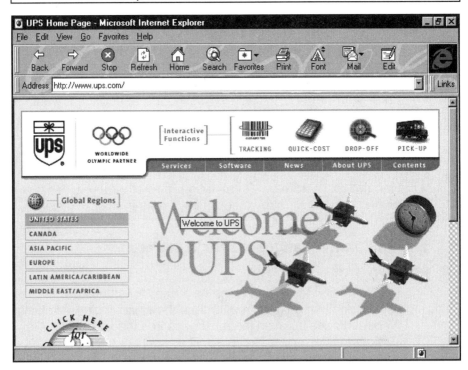

- The UPS Web site is simple and well organized—you can get to any of the most commonly used features with one click via the Interactive Functions icons. Click Tracking, enter a package tracking number, and then click Track to find the location of a package. Click Quick Cost and enter the requested delivery and package information to find out the cost of shipping a package via a particular service. A list of costs for other UPS services is also supplied so that you can decide whether the extra cost of getting the package to its destination faster is worthwhile.

- Click Drop-Off to find the UPS drop-off locations nearest you. Enter the location you want to check and then click Search Locations. A map showing your location and the five nearest drop-off sites will appear. You can include self-service sites, staffed sites, or both in your location search.

- Click Pick-Up to schedule a UPS package pickup. The UPS site even has an icon for updated information on the status of ongoing UPS labor negotiations.

FedEx

http://www.fedex.com

 A quick way to open an account with FedEx, track packages, get rate information, and prepare a package for shipment.

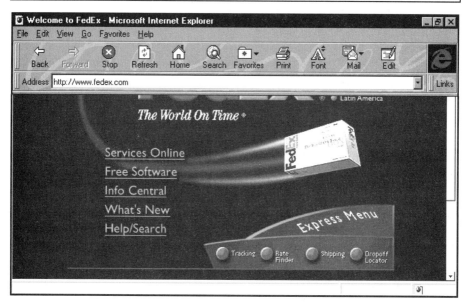

- This well-organized site lets you turn your computer into a full-fledged shipping station. Use the home page's Express Menu to jump to pages for tracking packages, finding rates (very important now that

FedEx has moved to zone-based shipping charges), preparing packages for shipping, and finding the nearest drop-off location.

- Though finding a drop-off location is important if you're on the road and need to find a drop box fast, the Dropoff Locator merely states that there are over 40,000 convenient locations to drop off a package. It does, however, list partner businesses such as Kinko's and OfficeMax where FedEx drop boxes are located. So, if you know where a store for one of the partner businesses on the list is, you're in luck. You can also use supplied links to jump to the Web sites for these associated businesses.

- The Tracking service is easy to use. Just enter the airbill number for the package you want to track and the destination country, then click and let the software do the work. You can also use Advanced Tracking if you know the account to which number the package was billed.

- Perhaps the most useful service on the FedEx site is the InterNetShip page, which enables you to prepare a package airbill and print it, complete with a FedEx barcode, using your computer and laser printer. Simply enter your FedEx account number and a net User ID which you can obtain from the site, then enter the shipping and addressee information and print your airbill. You can also request a pickup from this part of the site and notify the recipient that you are sending the package via e-mail.

Other Sites

United States Postal Service

http://www.usps.com

- Track express packages, send the postal service change of address information, link to apply for a U.S. passport, calculate postage, and locate the nearest post office to a location.

DHL

http://www.dhl.com

- This site allows you to track DHL express packages using Airwaybill numbers, but it doesn't offer much in the way of other online services.

Find Tax Information

◆ **IRS Digital Daily** ◆ **TaxResources** ◆ **TaxLibrary.Com** ◆**Other Sites**

Check these sites if you prepare your own taxes, prepare returns for your business, or if you need to keep informed about the latest updates to tax legislation. You can find tax forms online and even file your return electronically via the official IRS Digital Daily site.

IRS Digital Daily

http://www.irs.ustreas.gov/prod/cover.html

 Official Internal Revenue Service Web site provides a wealth of forms, publications, and information about filing your taxes.

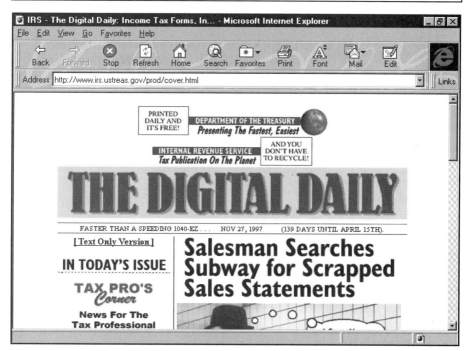

- It's easy not to like the Internal Revenue Service. No one likes to pay taxes, but you can admire the IRS Web site called The Digital Daily, which provides a great deal of help in getting through the annual ordeal of preparing those wordy, maze-like tax forms.

- The Digital Daily provides advice for tax professionals that even amateurs who like to file their own returns can use. You can also click on links that highlight the latest news in tax legislation.

- Often, a major last-minute tax preparation snag is not having the right form or schedule. Now you can click on the Forms and Publications link at The Digital Daily to browse more than twenty IRS publications online. You can then click the Publications or Forms and Instructions link to download the files you want. Use search tools to find the file you need and even locate forms from previous years.

- If you're having a problem dealing with the IRS, you can click on the Taxpayer Advocate link. Use this service to find out your rights as a taxpayer or resolve a problem with an auditor.

- You can also click the Electronic Services link to access the IRS online filing tools.

TaxResources

http://www2.best.com/~ftmexpat/html/taxsites.html

 Thorough directory of online tax resources bolstered by comments and pointers from the Web page author.

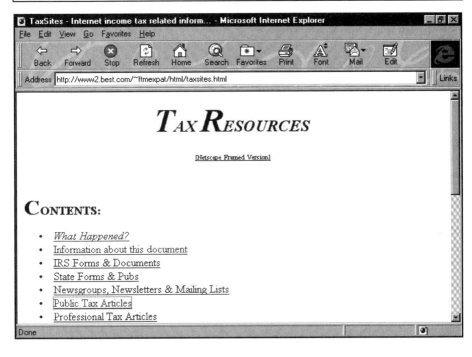

- TaxResources is a great site for managers who want to stay on top of the latest tax news. The site offers a directory of online tax resources along with commentary about the various links by the Web site's author, Frank McNeil.

- TaxResources includes almost two dozen general information categories. Click on one of these links to see topical links and the author's comments and advice about how to use them.

- The primary advantage of using this site is using the small tips and pointers the author provides as you conduct your search. For example, clicking on the What Happened link shows you a page of links to tools the author uses to stay apprised of new developments in tax law.

- Having someone to point the way in the world of online tax information is an outstanding value provided free of charge at this site.

TaxLibrary.Com

http://www.taxlibrary.com/TaxLibrary/HomePage.nsf

 This online research site for tax professionals requires a subscription fee. Benefits to users include research carrels for storing bookmarked case documents as well as online updates for changes to pertinent code.

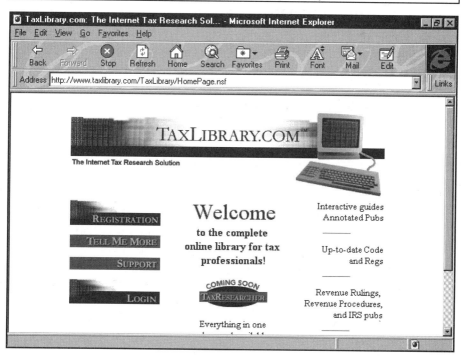

- TaxLibrary.Com is an authoritative online tax research library for accountants, tax preparers, and attorneys. This site is a service of Thompson Publishing Group, Inc., and requires a subscription fee of $30 per month or $300 per year.

- TaxLibrary.Com provides tax professionals with a complete resource for researching tax questions. The site provides searchable and browsable up-to-date tax code as well as the option of having a professional tax researcher find the information you need.

- The Alerts and Reminders service keeps you apprised of code and regulations changes. You can view code additions, amendments highlighted in green, and code deletions highlighted with red strikethrough.

- The Personal Carrel link enables you to organize your research by collecting bookmarks to documents you want to find again, organize bookmarks into client or case folders, add personal notes to bookmarks, and request e-mail alerts regarding documents you collect.

Other Sites

U.S. Internal Revenue Code

http://www.fourmilab.ch/ustax/www/contents.html

- This is it: The entire United States Tax Code online and complete with links to all of its various sections.

Essential Links Taxes

http://www.el.com/elinks/taxes/

- This is the tax page of the Essential Links Web site, an outstanding starting point for any online search for tax resources. Includes dozens of tax Web site links.

$5 Tax Tip

http://www.frontiernet.net/~pjones/taxtip.htm

- Submit specific tax questions to this network of experts. The fee for an answer is only $5. Good practical advice from this site can mean the difference between filing your own return and paying a preparer, but remember, you get what you pay for.

Find Legal Advice

◆ **West's Legal Directory** ◆ **FindLaw** ◆ **Hieros Gamos**
◆ **Legal Information Institute** ◆ **Other Sites**

Legal advice is expensive, unless you find it on the Web. Dozens of legal research Web sites can help you find the answers to your legal questions without consulting an attorney—or at least tell you the right attorney to consult. Use these sites to check the actual text of laws and regulations, review court rulings and case precedents, and contact all types of legal advisors.

West's Legal Directory

http://www.wld.com

 Search the directories and databases of West Group, the world's leading provider of legal information.

- Part of the West Group's Web site, West's Legal Directory provides an outstanding resource for business people who need to find legal assistance. West Group is the leading provider of information to the legal industry, but the West Web site also includes links and search tools that can benefit you.

- The Law Information Center is designed to help non-legal browsers find the information they need. Click on links that provide advice such as "Get tips on how to hire a lawyer," and "Read articles on 42 legal topics from West's Encyclopedia of American Law."
- You can also search for a lawyer or firm in West's Legal Directory. The database includes more than 800,000 listings.
- Click Public Information from the KnowX link to access public records about corporations, bankruptcies, property transfers, and other legal documents that can help you research a client or competitor.

FindLaw

http://www.findlaw.com

 Use the most complete directory and search Web site for the legal profession to find answers to your legal questions.

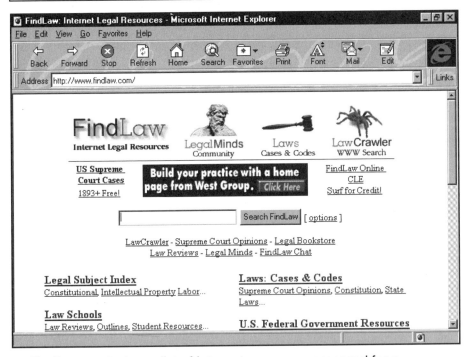

- FindLaw started as a list of Internet resources prepared for a workshop of the Northern California Law Librarians. It has evolved into an award-winning search and directory Web site for legal research.

- Modeled on the user interface design pioneered by the Yahoo! directory site, FindLaw lets you research whatever legal topic you have in mind by drilling down into more specific layers of information and links.

- FindLaw also features several tools in clickable icons along the top of the page. Click LawCrawler to search the complete database of FindLaw sites using the AltaVista search engine.

- Click Laws: Cases & Codes to see category links to cases and court decisions. Click LegalMinds–Community to see links to various resources including legal reference, education information, classifieds, organizations, bulletins, and other legal subjects.

Hieros Gamos

http://www.hg.org/hg.html

 This comprehensive resource and directory site rivals other top legal search and directory sites for completeness.

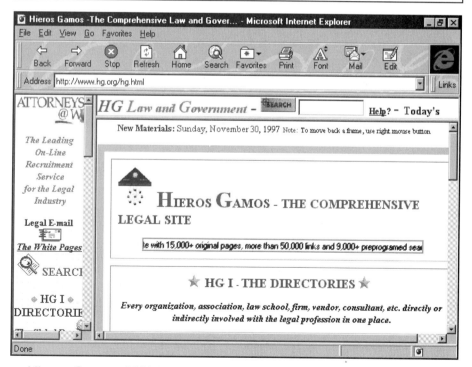

- Hieros Gamos (HG) is one of the most comprehensive legal sites on the Web, claiming directory listings for "every organization, association, law school, firm, vendor, consultant . . . involved with the legal profession in one place." It's a lofty claim, but the HG site may come very close to achieving it.

- The HG site is divided into three main sections. HG I is the directory portion of the site, split into a dozen categories, including bar associations, law firms, dispute resolution, and associated services. Click one of the category links to narrow your search or enter the topic you want to find in the search engine text box.

- The HG II portion of the site is a very complete directory of the worldwide practice of law divided into 70 primary practice areas and 130 additional areas. The directory topics are organized alphabetically.

- HG III includes links to global legal resource guides, including employment, publications, U.S. courts & cases, and process servers.

- While the Hieros Gamos site is very complete, its organization makes it somewhat difficult to use. Skip the directory categories and cut to the chase by entering your topic in the search engine text box. You'll probably find the information you need.

Legal Information Institute
http://www.law.cornell.edu/lii.table.html

 The Cornell Law School provides this superb resource for in-depth legal research.

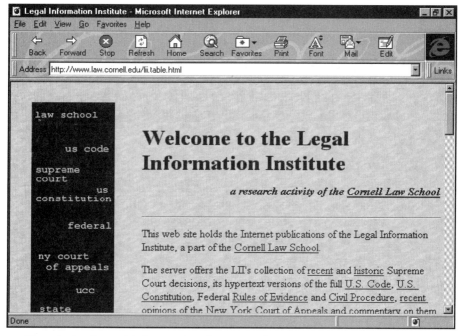

- Check the Legal Information Institute (LII) Web site for another outstanding collection of law resources. The Institute is a service of the Cornell Law School and contains a wide variety of services for finding the legal information you need.

- For example, you can search the LII list of topic summary links to primary source material either via an alphabetical listing of topics or a searchable index.

- Click the Supreme Court link to search summaries of recent and historic decisions. Click the Constitution link to see a hyperlinked version of the complete document.

- The State link includes legal documents and information from all 50 states. The Federal and World links telescope in to topic links in the LII database.

- Use the LII as a great free supplement to any legal research your business needs.

Other Sites

Corporate Agents, Inc.

http://www.corporate.com/cover_f.html

- Incorporate your business in any state online with this fast, easy service.

Center for Information Law and Policy

http://www.law.vill.edu/

- A clearinghouse for legal information provided by the Villanova University School of Law and Illinois Institute of Technology's Kent College of Law. Good source of links to international law and dispute resolution resources.

American Bankruptcy Institute

http://www.abiworld.org/

- Premier site for information on bankruptcy law. Find a certified bankruptcy specialist or access the institute's Association of Turnaround Professionals who provide turnaround, crisis management, and restructuring of troubled businesses.

Quickforms Contracts

http://www.quickforms.com

- For $20 you can draft a new contract online using boilerplate documents supplied by QuickForms software.

Consult Government Agencies

◆ FedWorld Information Network
◆ Thomas ◆ CBDNet ◆Other Sites

When you need to find something or someone in the federal government, you often find yourself faced with a maze of bureaus, agencies, departments, and red tape. These Web sites can help you cut through the bureaucracy and locate what you need to research laws or regulations, apply for government services or contracts, register your intellectual property, or simply keep up to date with Congressional activities.

FedWorld Information Network

http://www.fedworld.gov

 Search more than 300,000 government information products and get the latest government job postings.

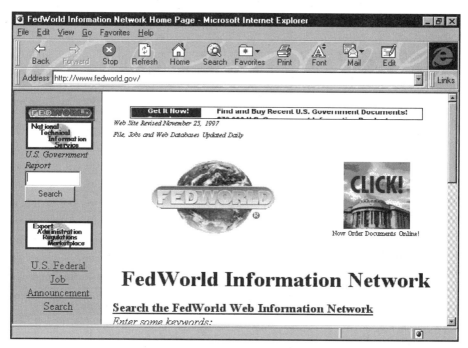

- Start your search for government information with FedWorld, a directory site administered by the National Technical Information

Service of the U.S. Department of Commerce. FedWorld is the best place to look for information produced by or about the U.S. federal government, including regulations, articles, job opportunities, and searchable databases.

- Click on the U.S. Business Advisor link to access the government's chief source of information for business. Here you can get answers to common questions that businesses ask the government, how-to guides and tools, a search engine for regulations and information, and a browse page containing government sites organized by topic.

Thomas

http://thomas.loc.gov

 Follow the current activities of the U.S. Congress and research past federal legislation. This site includes complete directories of the Senate and the House of Representatives.

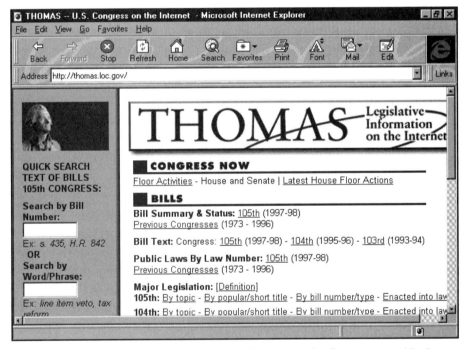

- Keep up to date on legislative developments in Congress with the Thomas Web site. A service of the Library of Congress named after Thomas Jefferson, this Web site is the ultimate source for information about the activities of both the U.S. Senate and the House of Representatives.

- Use the Thomas search engine to search several databases, including the current week's floor activities of Congress as well as text, summaries, and/or activities surrounding current and historical bills (historical meaning prior to 1973).

- Other searchable databases include Congressional Record text and index, Congressional committee reports and home pages, and historical documents (important documents from the founding of the United States).

- You can also find articles describing the legislative process, and links to Internet resources for government entities such as the House and Senate Web pages, Library of Congress, General Accounting Office, and Congressional Budget Office.

CBDNet

http://cbdnet.access.gpo.gov/index.html

 Find government contract opportunities by searching the Department of Commerce database of procurement notices.

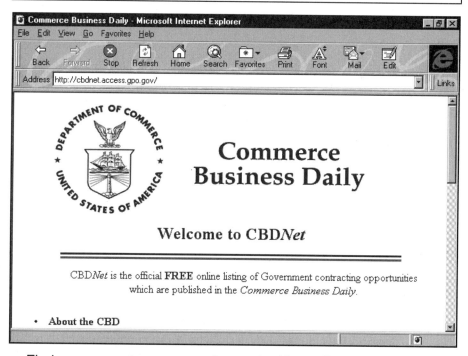

- Find government procurement opportunities online at the Commerce Business Daily (CBD) page, CBDNet, part of the

Department of Commerce Web site. CBD regularly updates a database of government procurements, contract awards, and sales of government property.

- Search CBDNet to find opportunities for doing business with the federal government. All proposed government contracts and procurements over $25,000 are required by law to be listed in the CBD database.

- You can conduct either a simple search or a fielded search of the CBD database. For a simple search, you only need to enter a keyword or keywords. Use the fielded search if you want to look up specific segments of the CBD database or if you want to use operators to narrow your search criteria.

- The CBD database contains all active notices of government contract requisitions. The database is updated continuously with new requisitions. Notices of requisition remain in the active database for 15 days, after which they are moved permanently to an archive database. You can also include the archive database in your searches.

- After you receive search results, you can click links to see the actual procurement notice text.

Other Sites

Federal Web Locator

http://www.law.vill.edu/Fed-Agency/fedwebloc.html

- This clearinghouse directory of federal information and resources is provided by the Villanova Center for Information Law and Policy. It includes a well-organized index of links to all government agency and department Web sites.

FedLaw

http://www.legal.gsa.gov/

- This is the complete hyperlinked text of federal laws and regulations. You can search the complete text of the U.S. Code by title and section.

Government Information Exchange

http://www.info.gov/Info/html/phone_directories.htm

- This site indexes links for phone directories of all branches, departments, and agencies of the federal government. The Federal Yellow Pages at this site includes links to all government departments, agencies, and services.

Consult OSHA Regulations

◆ **OSHA Web Site** ◆ **OSHA Computerized Information System**
◆ **Other Sites**

Managers, small business owners, and human resources staff often need to consult the latest OSHA regulations updates to help make decisions regarding personnel and work safety issues. The sites profiled here provide the definitive online sources for finding the information you need when you have a question about OSHA programs, regulations, and compliance.

OSHA Web Site

http://www.osha.gov

 The official source for comprehensive information about OSHA regulations and compliance programs.

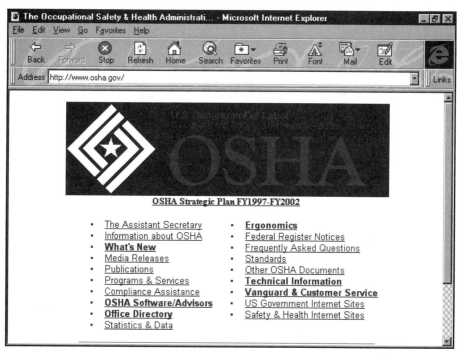

- Go straight to the source to find the most complete collection of information about OSHA regulations. The OSHA Web site, part of the larger U.S. Department of Labor Web site, provides quick answers to your questions about OSHA compliance.

- Check the Frequently Asked Questions link for concise information about the most common OSHA questions you may have.

- Click on the very valuable Compliance Assistance link to learn what regulations are of most common concern for your industry and size of business. You can use the Most Frequently Violated Standards tool to search by number of employees, federal or state jurisdiction, and Standard Industrial Classification code (SIC). You can also find which SIC code has the most violations for a federal or state OSHA standard.

OSHA Computerized Information System

http://www.osha-slc.gov/

 Use the directories and search engine provided by this OSHA site to help you quickly find answers to questions about OSHA programs and regulations.

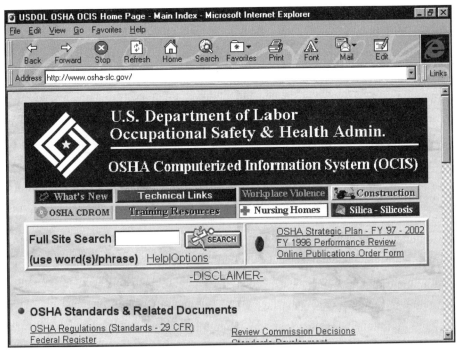

- The OSHA Computerized Information Services is another portion of the Department of Labor's online OSHA resources. This site is maintained by OSHA's Salt Lake City office, and provides additional organization of OSHA resources that can help you quickly find the answers and information you need.

- The home page for this site includes links to specific topic areas such as Technical Links, Workplace Violence, Construction, and Training Resources. The Full Site Search feature, also available from the home page, allows you to enter keywords to find the information you need.

- The home page provides a helpful, organized directory of OSHA links, under categories such as OSHA Standards & Related Documents, New Initiatives and Special Emphasis Programs, Training and Registration, and OSHA Programs and Offices.

- Though this site contains many of the same resources as the main OSHA Web site, the convenient search engine and the extra degree of organization may help you zero in on the information you need more quickly than at the general OSHA site.

Other Sites

CCOHS Health and Safety Directory

http://www.ccohs.ca/resources/hshome.html

- This extensive directory of nearly 1500 online health and safety resources is compiled and maintained by the Canadian Centre for Occupational Health and Safety.

NIOSH

http://www.cdc.gov/niosh/homepage.html

- The National Institute for Occupational Safety and Health was founded in 1970 as part of the Centers for Disease Control and Prevention (CDC). Check this site to learn about the many NIOSH activities and educational programs.

U.S. Department of Labor

http://www.dol.gov

- The U.S. Department of Labor Web site includes information about minimum wage requirements, labor statutory and regulatory information, labor-related data and statistics, grant and contract information, as well as information about welfare-to-work programs and small business retirement solutions.

Find Venture Capital

◆ **MoneyHunter** ◆ **Federal Money Retriever**
◆ **Venture Capital Resource Library** ◆ **Other Sites**

Find money to start or expand your business at these venture capital Web sites. These sites allow investors to find suitable businesses to finance. Some sites take a more active role and actively match investors to businesses seeking capital.

MoneyHunter

http://www.moneyhunter.com

 Web site of the popular MoneyHunt public TV show connects entrepreneurs and investors in a unique and entertaining way.

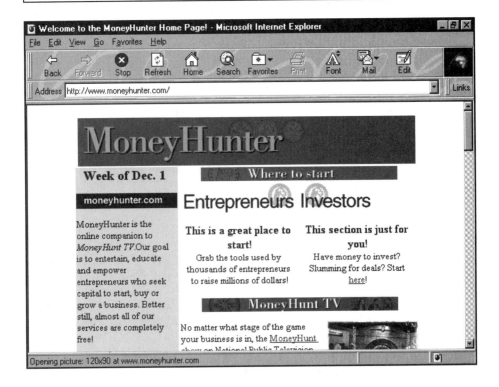

- MoneyHunter is the Web site of the National Public Television show the MoneyHunt. More than a million people tune in to the MoneyHunt each week to see entrepreneurs present their business plans to a panel of financial Siskel and Eberts, who either give the plans a big thumbs-up or a no-holds-barred skewering.

- The show is entertaining but has its serious side—last year 13 of 26 guest entrepreneurs garnered $17 million in capital after presenting their business plans on the air.

- The MoneyHunter Web site lets you tap into the expertise and exposure showcased on the TV show. If you're looking for investor dollars, click the Entrepreneur link and choose from a menu of outstanding resources.

- Click Business Plan Template to access a time-proven blueprint for writing a business plan that you can use to help win you capital investment funds. A quarter of a million entrepreneurs have used the plan template to present their businesses to potential investors.

- Click Golden Rolodex to search the MoneyHunter database of investors and fellow entrepreneurs. You can even click Online Audition to see if you have the right stuff to appear on the MoneyHunt TV show.

- MoneyHunter is also a great site for investors who are looking for hidden gems. Venture capitalists can search the Golden Rolodex, check out spotlighted companies, and take a peek at the Capital Calendar of upcoming venture capital events in their area.

Federal Money Retriever

http://www.idimagic.com/htmls/fed_mon2.html

 Visit this site to check out a sample of the top software package for finding federal grant funding.

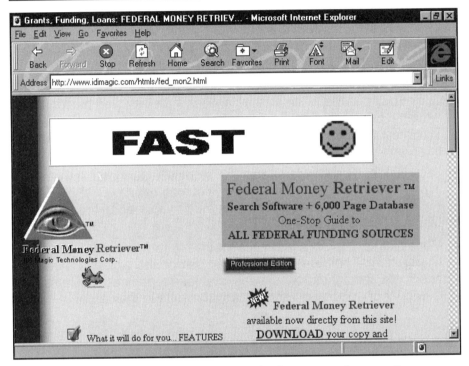

- The Federal Money Retriever Web site is not much more than an electronic brochure and storefront for IDI Magic Technology's Federal Money Retriever software package. However, the software is such a great resource for anyone looking to tap into the treasure trove of federal grant dollars that this site can't be skipped.

- Use the site to find out about the software, which lets you search a 6,000-page database of federal funding sources. This software makes it easy to sift through the tangled maze of federal agencies to find grant opportunities for your business or organization. If you like what you see, you can order and download the software directly from the Web page.

- The Web site also includes statistics culled from the Money Retriever database showing how many federal dollars go to whom.

212

Venture Capital Resource Library
http://www.vfinance.com

 Complete resource clearinghouse site for businesses looking for venture capital. Investors and business service providers can list their companies at this site free of charge.

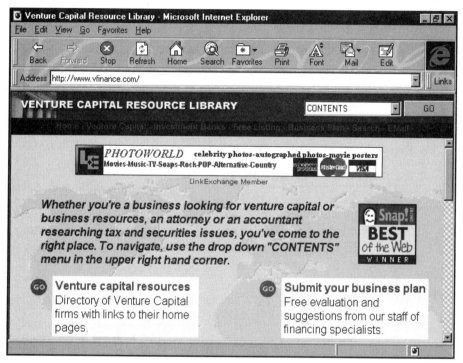

- The Venture Capital Resource Library provides a complete, get-down-to-business Web site to connect you with all the resources you need to find venture capital and financing.

- Click one of the Go buttons to link to a directory of venture capital firm links, use a free business plan template, or submit your business plan for free evaluation from the library's staff of financing experts.

- Use the convenient Go button and contents menu at the top of the home page to find a link to business resources ranging from commercial credit to currency converters. Many of these menu items link you to other Web sites.

- If you're looking for venture capital opportunities, click on the Initial Public Offerings Go button. This link connects you to IPOCentral, an outstanding Web site for keeping tabs on the latest in IPO news, including who's going public and where they are in the process.

- If you offer business services or financing, you can also register to submit your business for a free listing at the Resource Library section of the Web site.

Other Sites

DataMerge

http://www.datamerge.com/index.html

- The corporate Web site for DataMerge, Inc., offers various financial and business planning software products. Here you can find financing, register as a business lender in the DataMerge database, or check the cool business links page.

Venture Capital World Online

http://www.vcworld.com/vcw/index.html

- If you can ignore the fact that some of the pages on this international Web site are in Swedish, this is a worthwhile site to search for venture capital. Though the company that runs the site is based in Sweden, almost 40% of the site's users are from the United States.

M&A Marketplace

http://www.mergernetwork.com/

- M&A (stands for merger and acquisition) Marketplace is a top Web site for buying and selling businesses. You can search both the buyers and sellers databases free of charge, but you have to pay the membership fee to access contact information, perform advanced searches, and use smart agents for searching the database.

Develop Sales Leads

◆ **SalesLeads USA** ◆ **Thomas Register**
◆ **Forbes Annual Report on American Industry** ◆ **Other Sites**

You can use the Web to help you develop sales leads. Many sites include searchable databases of U.S. and international corporations, including company financial information and key contacts. The large databases and powerful search engines at these sites help you quickly zero in on the types of businesses you want to find.

SalesLeads USA

http://www.lookupusa.com/

Extensive database of sales leads that you can search to find and order company information.

- SalesLeads USA is a Web service offered by American Business Information. The site offers a searchable database of more than 10 million businesses and more than 100 million households. Though it's hard to determine how accurate these claims and the size of the databases are, suffice to say that there is a multitude of information about prospective customers at this site. A search of businesses in just one Zip Code returned a result of more than 2,400 businesses.

- Click the Sales Leads and Mailing Lists icon to access a search engine that you can use to search by business type, state, county, metropolitan area, city, Zip Code, or by company name. After you receive initial search results, you can further narrow your search by a number of different criteria, and then choose whether you want to pay for the list of business information at the quoted price.

- Click the Business Profiles and Credit Ratings icon to search the SalesLeads USA database of company profiles. This is an excellent source of corporate information, including estimated annual sales, name of owner or top decision-maker, credit rating code, number of employees, and more. Each profile you request costs $3.

- Click on the Sales Leads products link at the home page to see a directory listing of links to each of the site's sales lead formats, including prospect lists, mailing labels, diskettes and magnetic tape, and monthly sales lead updates.

Thomas Register

http://www2.thomasregister.com/index.cgi?balancing

 Search the Thomas Register database of more than 150,000 companies free of charge. Listing your company and searching the database are both available here at no cost.

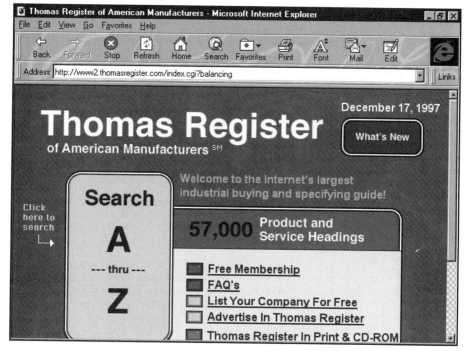

- The Thomas Register Web site provides a search engine for its database of information on more than 150,000 companies in more than 57,000 product and service headings.

- You can search the database and list your company in the database free of charge.

- The site is straightforward and easy to use. Simply click on the Search A to Z graphic, enter your ID and password, then start hunting. Site membership is free, but you have to register to search.

- The search engine is powerful, allowing you to modify search results by geographical specifications or by detailed product descriptions. You can also easily access 3,100 online supplier catalogs and links to 800 company Web sites through the Thomas Register database.

Forbes Annual Report on American Industry

http://www.forbes.com/jan1/search.htm

 Search the Forbes database of companies surveyed in its annual report on American industry. Detailed financial information on companies listed in the database is available here free of charge.

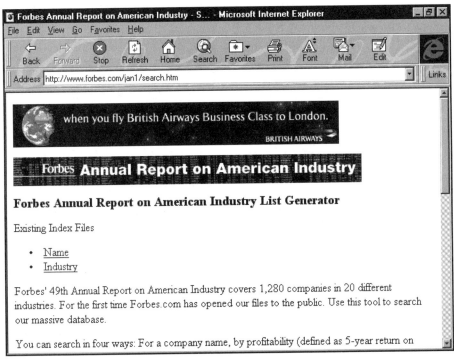

- In 1997, Forbes opened its annual report on American business and industry to the public free of charge. Use this Web site to search the database of more than 1,200 companies by name or industry.

- Click on the Industry link to see a page that has a chart breaking industries down by Profitability, Sales Growth, and Earnings Growth. Click on an industry link to see further sub-categories.

- For example, clicking on Construction takes you to a list of company links divided into the sub-categories Commercial Builders, Residential Builders, Cement and Gypsum, and Other Materials. Company links are displayed along with statistics for Five-Year Price Change, Recent Price, and EPS 1997 Estimate Dollars.

- If you already know the company you want to find, click the Name link. This takes you to an alphabetical index of the company database. Click the appropriate letter to look for the company you want. Company listings include financial information such as sales, net income, profit margin, and debt/capital ratios.

Other Sites

Dun & Bradstreet Companies Online

http://www.companiesonline.com/

- Search for information in Dun & Bradstreet's database of more than 100,000 public and private companies. The site also includes a directory listing of business categories that you can use to drill into the database to search for companies in a particular industry.

Inc. 500

http://www.inc.com/500/1997.html

- Search the Inc. magazine list of its top 500 companies. The database can be searched by company name, by descriptive keywords, by state, or by business sector.

Fortune 500

http://pathfinder.com/@@mAGEbAcAb6qkVnW7/fortune/fortune500/500list.html

- Search a database of the most famous "500" business list of all: the Fortune 500. This page can be found at the Fortune Magazine site through the Pathfinder online service. The site is well organized, with many links that help you browse the list of companies in various ways.

Market Your Product on the Web

◆ **Web Marketing Info Center** ◆ **The Home Page Maker**
◆ **CIO WebBusiness** ◆ **LinkExchange** ◆ **Other Sites**

Leverage the marketing power of the Web by consulting these sites. Free instruction and advice as well as professional fee-based services are available to help you set up shop online successfully.

Web Marketing Info Center

http://www.wilsonweb.com/webmarket/

 The place to go for the best collection of Web marketing and site building resources and information.

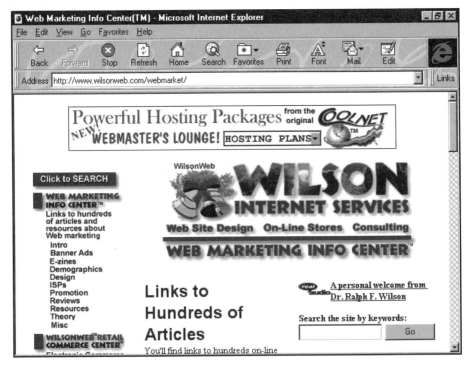

- Getting started is often the hardest part of any undertaking, and the same holds true for marketing your products or services on the Web. Unless your company is large enough to hire an outside firm to launch and manage your site, the technical aspects of creating a corporate home page can be daunting.

- In addition, once you get past the initial task of getting a site up and running, you're faced with the challenge of getting the site noticed and generating traffic and sales.

- The Web Marketing Info Center is perhaps the top resource available on the Web for meeting these challenges head on. The people at Wilson Internet Services, a Web page design and consulting firm, have compiled a comprehensive collection of articles and resources to help you find the information you need to market your company on the Web.

- The Web Marketing Info Center page is thoughtfully organized to help you find the right resources. A link directory appears at the right of the page, including such topics as Banner Advertising Models, Branding on the Web, and Demographics of the Web. Click one of these topic links to browse a page devoted to the subject, complete with many links to associated articles.

- Another series of topical links is displayed at the left of the Marketing Info Center home page. There are dozens of category links here that take you to dozens of articles on each subject.

- If you're just starting out and the array of choices available on the Web Marketing Info Center page seems a little overwhelming, scroll down the page to find four links to good introductory articles.

- Another bonus of checking out this Web page: If you like what you see here, you can contact Wilson Internet Services to have them start helping you build your site.

The Home Page Maker

http://www.wizard.com/~fifi/pagemake.html

Create a quick and easy Web page for yourself or for your business using this site. Simple instructions walk you through entering information and choosing page design elements.

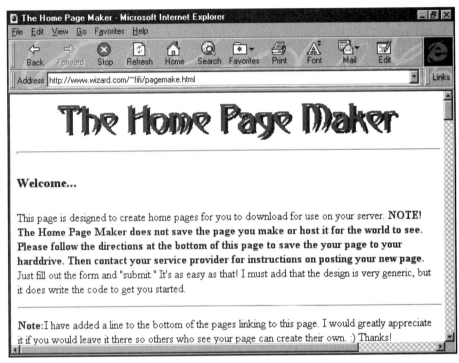

- If you want to get started right away with a quick home page for your business or yourself and you don't have the time to invest in learning how to program HTML, try using The Home Page Maker.

- This handy site, prepared by an individual and available free of charge, walks you through a simple input form for entering your personal and/or business information. Then you enter a few favorite places on the Web that can be included as links on your page.

- After you enter your basic information into the form, you can select colors for the various text and graphical elements of your page. Remember to keep the color scheme simple and avoid using too many fonts and graphical elements.

222

- Finally, you can enter a famous quote or some words of wisdom you want to appear on your new Web page. Perhaps a company slogan or marketing phrase can go here.

- Click the Make My Page button to create the code for your Web page. Note that you must save the page to your computer system yourself. The Home Page Maker site does not automatically do that for you.

CIO WebBusiness

http://webbusiness.cio.com

 Satisfy the gearhead in you by checking out the latest in Webmaster shoptalk at CIO WebBusiness.

- If you're a professional Webmaster or if you just want to read about what the pros do, check out the CIO WebBusiness page for high-powered information on designing and maintaining a corporate Web site.

- CIO Magazine is a trade publication for information technology professionals. The complete online version of the magazine can be accessed by clicking on the CIO Magazine link at the left of the page.

- Click on one of the WebBusiness Research Center links to learn about the challenges of life as a professional Webmaster. Each page is loaded with links to in-depth and highly technical information, from articles to features to white papers.
- Click on links to other resources such as Web Professional Wanted, Webmaster Archives, and Web Events. Feature articles from the current issue of CIO Magazine are also available.

LinkExchange

http://www.linkexchange.com

 This free service puts you in touch with more than 200,000 Web sites with which you can exchange Web links and advertising space to improve your exposure on the Web.

- Visit this top site for generating hits at your company Web site. LinkExchange puts its members in contact with each other so that they can exchange advertising and links on each other's Web sites.

- The idea is simple, but powerful. The more ads exchanged, the greater the likelihood of someone clicking on your site. What's more, you're generating additional exposure by essentially giving away something that doesn't cost you anything but space on your page.

- Webmaster membership at LinkExchange is free upon registration. Membership allows you to exchange ads with other members, purchase targeted Web advertising packages, and search the database of more than 200,000 members.

- Member or not, you can click on the Resources for Web site owners link to get information for improving the design and traffic flow at your Web site.

Other Sites

Website Promoter's Resource Center

http://www.wprc.com/

- This top site for improving traffic to your Web site includes resources and information on banner advertising, URL submission, targeted e-mail, and press releases.

Relevant Knowledge

http://www.relevantknowledge.com

- Relevant Knowledge will help you track and measure your Web site's audience. How many people are you reaching online? Who are they, and will they buy anything from you? Relevant Knowledge can tell you the answers—but for a fee.

Mouse Tracks

http://nsns.com/MouseTracks/

- Mouse Tracks is a good site to check for periodic updates on trends and developments in Web marketing. Includes links to conferences, articles, and commentary online.

Develop Direct Marketing Online

◆ **Eagle Direct Marketing** ◆ **American List Counsel**
◆ **PostMaster Direct Response** ◆ **Other Sites**

The ability to search databases and send messages online makes the Web a perfect place to develop direct marketing campaigns. Find sites that have searchable mailing lists or direct e-mail services that can help you cut mailing costs and hit your target market.

Eagle Direct Marketing

http://eagle.multiactive.com/

 Eagle provides a sample search that shows the power of narrowing direct marketing lists online.

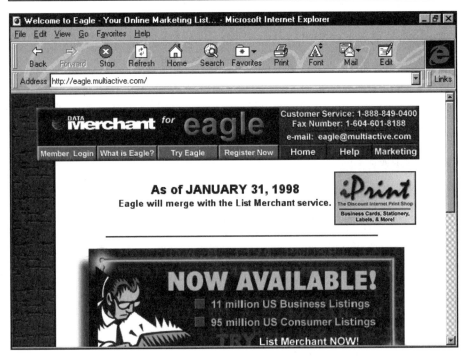

- The Eagle Direct Marketing site provides a good example of the type of direct marketing services available on the Web.

- The power of database marketing on the Web is the speed with which you can access a variety of list providers and their lists. In many cases you can search direct marketing lists online before you buy, thus eliminating stale and inappropriate listings and lowering your cost.

- Click on the Try Eagle link to conduct a sample search of one of Eagle's databases according to criteria you enter. This demonstration will give you an idea of the powerful service online list providers can offer.

- At the Eagle site, you can register to search and narrow its lists for free. Then, when you have a list that meets your needs, you pay only for the listings you have selected.

American List Counsel

http://www.amlist.com

 Find searchable lists and great information about direct mail marketing.

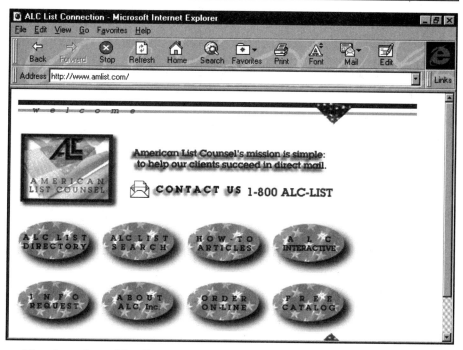

- The American List Counsel provides another example of direct marketing services available online.

- Click on the ALC List Directory icon to see a directory of links to available lists that you can browse by SIC (Standard Industrial Classification) code or by category. Click on the ALC List Search to perform a keyword search of the lists. Search results show ALC lists that match your entry.

- Click on the How-To Articles to see a listing of links to some very good information and tips about direct mail marketing.

PostMaster Direct Response

http://www.postmasterdirect.com/welcome.mhtml

 Hit your target market online with direct e-mail marketing.

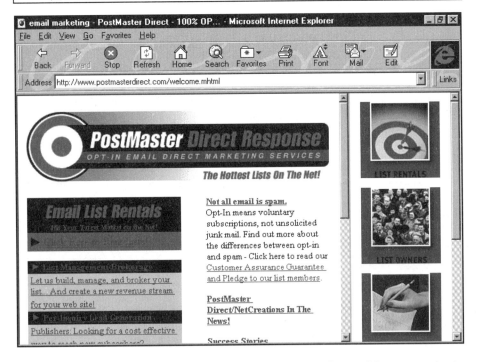

- Direct marketing works just as well using e-mail as with paper. Just be careful to avoid what's commonly called *spamming* on the Web. Spamming is the unsolicited delivery of e-mail sales messages to a wide target audience.

228

- Spamming tends to generate a rather vehement backlash from some members of the Internet community, and it certainly is less effective than a well-targeted electronic mailing.

- Check sites such as PostMaster Direct Response to find what are called "opt-in" lists—lists of people who voluntarily request information about a particular topic. Messages sent from these lists are received in a kinder light in the online world and tend to receive a better response rate.

- PostMaster Direct Response services include per-inquiry lead generation, in which you pay for leads generated in response to a free sample or trial offer, and list management and brokerage.

Other Sites

Database America

http://www.databaseamerica.com/html/index.htm

- This online sales lead and direct marketing development site provides numerous services, including list services, computer services, and interactive media. Available lists include 11,000,000 businesses and 95 million households in target marketing databases.

targ*it e-mail

http://www.targ-it.com/index.htm

- Purchase targeted e-mail lists for use in your online direct marketing campaigns. targ*it e-mail provides lists of more than 40,000 Webmasters, more than 50,000 online magazine subscribers, 75,000 business professionals, and 500,000 catalog shoppers. All lists on the targ*it site are opt-in lists, developed using information from people who have indicated a desire to be receive mail about a particular topic.

Sell Your Products in Other Countries

◆ **International Business Resources on the WWW**
◆ **NAFTAnet** ◆ **Other Sites**

Expand your markets by exporting your product to other countries with the help of these sites. The two featured sites provide excellent search and directory starting points for finding international trade resources online. Other sites help you make contacts with import/export partners overseas.

International Business Resources on the WWW

http://ciber.bus.msu.edu/busres.htm

 Start your quest for information about expanding your global sales presence here. This is the top search and directory site for research on international trade.

- The best place to start your search for help in international sales is the International Business Resources on the WWW site, produced

230

by Michigan State University's Center for International Business Education and Research. This is a superb directory site for finding online information and business links about international trade. The site has received a number of awards from online and computer magazines.

- Like most good directory sites, you can either search or browse to find what you want. Type keywords in the search textbox and click on the Search Now! button.

- Scroll down the home page to browse the index of about twenty category links. Click on a link that interests you to see a page of Web site links for that topic along with a brief description of each site.

NAFTAnet

http://www.nafta.net

Find opportunities for expanding your markets in Mexico and Canada at this excellent directory site produced with the bottom line in mind.

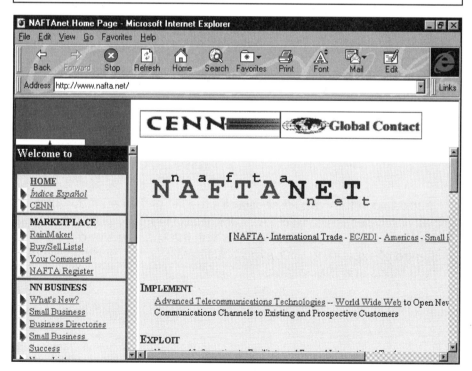

- How can you take advantage of trade opportunities that may be available due to NAFTA, the North American Free Trade Agreement? One of the best ways to find out is to consult NAFTAnet, a directory site listing links to dozens of sites pertaining to trade with our neighbors to the north and south.

- Links on the main section of the home page are organized according to ways you can take advantage of NAFTA to grow your business.

- Click the Advanced Telecommunications Technologies—World Wide Web link to learn more about using the Web to reach NAFTA trading partners.

- Click the Exploit links for pertinent news articles, legal information, and other market and industry updates.

- Click the Reduce links to learn more about clearance, security, commercial technology, and ways to save time and money while doing business on the Internet.

- Go to the Target links to gather statistics about the impact of NAFTA trade and learn which industries are benefiting from NAFTA.

- Use the Welcome To menu at the left of the home page to click on bottom-line oriented topics such as Rainmaker, Buy/Sell Lists, Small Business Success, and $Market, the site's Marketplace section.

- Click on the NAFTA link near the top of the home page to see the entire text of the agreement as well as useful links to the NAFTA Implementation Resource Guide and the NAFTA Impact Update. You can also find out about GATT, the General Agreement on Tariffs and Trade, in this section of the directory.

- Check also in the NAFTA section for the list of Top 40 Industries that Will Benefit from NAFTA, prepared by the U.S. Department of Commerce. If your industry appears on the list, you stand a good chance of expanding your export business due to the reduction of trade tariffs and regulations.

Other Sites

BusinessEurope

http://www.businesseurope.com

- Search this site by country to find American Embassy reports, trade fair information, a trade bulletin board, and articles about trade in Europe.

International Business List

http://www.earthone.com/internat.html

- This Web site provides a place where business people can meet to make contacts and find new trading partners. It also features a message center for those seeking jobs, consultants, or other international business services.

World Access Network Direct

http://www.wand.com

- This site matches buyers and sellers in the global import/export trade. Search the database of postings by SIC or Harmonized Code, or by manufacturer. After you locate a match for your needs, WAND supplies contact information.

The CIA World Factbook

http://www.odci.gov/cia/publications/nsolo/wfb-all.htm

- Usually not known for giving away its information, the CIA supplies a full helping of its "intelligence" at this Web site. Search here for all kinds of statistical and cultural information about countries, regions, and populations around the world. Information is indexed alphabetically for easy searching. Be sure to view this site's great maps.

Appendix A: Essential Downloads

◆ Internet Explorer ◆ Netscape Navigator ◆ TUCOWS
◆ Shareware.Com ◆ The Jumbo Download Network
◆ VDOLive Video Player ◆ Adobe Acrobat Reader ◆ Shockwave

The Internet can be a convenient source for downloading valuable software. Log on to the following URLs to download Web and multimedia software, much of which is available free of charge or as shareware, which requires a minimal registration fee.

Internet Explorer

http://www.microsoft.com/ie/download/

- Internet Explorer 4.0 is the latest version of Microsoft's Internet browser software. It has attracted a lot of attention for both it's powerful new features and it's role in the Department of Justice investigation of Microsoft for antitrust violations.

- Explorer 4.0's active desktop features allow the browser software to be much more integrated into the Windows operating system you use to run your computer.

- You can also receive active content from the Web using Explorer's "push" technology. Active content lets you choose from among several Web content "channels" to receive automatic information updates to your desktop.

- Other Explorer 4.0 tools include NetMeeting virtual conferencing software and FrontPage Express. NetMeeting helps facilitate virtual meetings held via the Internet and one-to-one telephone calls from your computer. FrontPage Express enables you to create and post your own Web pages.

- Whatever the outcome of the legal wrangling, Explorer is rapidly gaining market acceptance as the leading Web browser. Get your copy free of charge at this site.

Netscape Navigator

http://home.netscape.com/download/index.html

- Netscape Navigator 4.0 is the other major Web browser on the market today and the direct descendant of the Mosaic browser that first swept many users into the world of surfing the Web.

- Netscape Communicator includes Navigator 4.0 and a complete suite of Internet tools, including Messenger for e-mail, Collabra for newsgroups, and Composer for creating Web pages.

- You can also download a complete installation of Netscape Communicator which includes Netscape Netcaster for receiving active channel content, Netscape Conference for online collaboration and the capability to handle rich multimedia content as well as bitstream fonts.

- Though you must pay for Netscape products available at this download site, you can download evaluation versions of new software free of charge. Educational institutions and nonprofit organizations can download a number of Netscape products at no charge.

TUCOWS

http://www.tucows.com

- TUCOWS stands for The Ultimate Collection Of Winsock Software. The site bills itself as the world's best collection of Internet software.

- After logging on to the TUCOWS home page, click the appropriate link for your geographical location (such as United States, Europe, Canada), then click the appropriate state (or other area) link. These geographical links are used to produce faster and more reliable software downloads.

- Next click the appropriate link for your computer's operating system. You will see a directory page listing links for more than 60 different types of Internet software.

- Click on a category link to see a listing of software available in that category for downloading. Listings include a complete description of the software, its hardware requirements, and a rating of the software (by number of cows). Click the Download button next to a particular listing to start downloading.

- Most software available at TUCOWS is either shareware or freeware, though some products offered are only demo versions that may have limited features or time restraints.

Shareware.Com

http://www.shareware.com

- Shareware.Com is another great site for downloading software via the Web. The site is a service of the C/Net Web page, noted for its computer and technology news coverage.

- You can browse the site by clicking on the New Arrivals or Most Popular links, or you can simply enter the name of the software you hope to find in the search engine text box.

- Highlights of available shareware are shown on the home page. Click on a link to go to a description of the shareware and a link to the download page.

The Jumbo Download Network

http://www.jumbo.com

- Yet another great software downloading site is The Jumbo Download Network, which lists more than 250,000 shareware programs and links. Available software is conveniently organized by channels, including Business, Desktop, Internet, Utilities, Games, Entertainment, Developer, and Demo City, which offers the latest commercial demos so you can try before you buy.

VDOLive Video Player

http://www.vdo.net/download/

- Download VDOnet Corporation's VDOLive Video Player 3.0 free of charge at this site. VDOLive is the top software for broadcasting and receiving video content over the Internet and is used by many major television networks, including CBS News, MTV, and PBS.

- Click on the VDOLive 3.0 link to begin downloading the software. You must register to download, but otherwise the procedure is free and relatively easy. Only the VDOLive Player software is available for free download. VDOLive server software must be purchased.

- You can also download a trial version of VDOPhone, touted as the first full-color video telephone available for either regular telephone lines or the Internet. VDOPhone lets you see and hear anyone over the Internet with no additional phone charges.

- VDOPhone is currently available for Windows 95 users only. The trial version expires after 5 hours of video reception.

Adobe Acrobat Reader

http://www.adobe.com

- Adobe Acrobat Reader lets you view, navigate, and print many document files available on the Web for downloading.

- To download the Acrobat Reader free of charge, click the Free Plug-Ins and Updates link at the Adobe home page. The link takes you to a file library page that displays a list of nearly thirty software products you can download. Links to download sites for each type of software are displayed by operating system.

- Click the Acrobat Reader link for your computer's operating system. The reader is available for Windows, Macintosh, DOS, UNIX, and OS/2. You will go to a page including short description links and download links for the available versions of Acrobat Reader. Click the Download link to register and begin downloading.

- You can also click the Tryout Software link at the Adobe home page to see descriptions of Adobe's latest multimedia and graphics products as well as download links for trial versions.

Shockwave

http://www.macromedia.com/shockwave/download/

- Macromedia Shockwave facilitates smooth viewing of animation and multimedia over the Internet. Many Web browsers and online services such as Internet Explorer, Netscape Navigator, and AOL include Shockwave with their software.

- If you want to download Shockwave, go to the Shockwave Download Center at the above URL, and click the Get Shockwave link.

Appendix B: Timesaving Tools

◆ Financial Calculators ◆ Calculators Online
◆ Universal Currency Converter ◆ The Time Zones Page ◆ Naval Clock
◆ Fast Area Code Finder ◆ National Address and Zip+4 Browser

Use the Web tools listed here to save time by finding the answer to many common financial and mathematical questions. You can also get the correct time around the world with the Time Zones and Naval Clock sites.

Financial Calculators

http://www.moneyadvisor.com/calc/

- Have you ever wondered whether you should lease or purchase a car? How much money do you have to save to become a millionaire by the time you retire? How much rent can you afford?
- The financial calculators available at the Financial Calculators page of the TimeValue Software Web site provide a host of interesting and practical tools for finding the answer to your financial questions.
- The directory of calculator links includes categories such as Auto Loans & Leasing, Loans & Savings Calculators, General Financial Calculators, Mortgage Calculators, Insurance Calculators, Tax Calculators, and Just For Fun Calculators.

Calculators Online

http://www-sci.lib.uci.edu/HSG/RefCalculators.html

- Another calculator site at Martindale's "The Reference Desk" provides more than 5,300 calculators.
- Links to the calculators are arranged in an alphabetical index of categories and subtopics. Click on a link to use one of the calculators.
- Business categories include Home & Office, Finance, Management/Business, Insurance, Stocks, Bonds, Options, and Commodities & Futures.
- You can also find many calculators for practical matters such as clothing, arts and crafts, medical, and law. Numerous mathematics and science calculators are also available, from simple unit conversion calculators to astrophysics.

Universal Currency Converter

http://www.xe.net./currency/

- This simple and useful Web site does one thing only, but does it well—currency conversion. If, for example, you want to know how many French francs you can get for $100, turn to this Web page.

- Type the amount of currency you want to convert, then select the type of currency (e.g., U.S. dollars). Next, select the type of currency you're converting to (e.g., French francs), and click the Perform Currency Conversion button.

- The Currency Converter tells you that $100 converts to 596.90 French francs. (Note that currency exchange rates fluctuate and converting currency usually requires a fee.)

The Time Zone Page

http://www.west.net/~lindley/zone/

- Another simple but very useful site is the Time Zone Page. Find the current time for more than 600 cities around the world.

- Select a city from the menu, then click Get the Time!

Naval Clock

http://tycho.usno.navy.mil/cgi-bin/timer.pl

- To check the most accurate clock available, go to the Naval Clock Web site. The site displays the current time in all North American time zones as well as Universal Time (also called Greenwich Mean Time).

Fast Area Code Finder

http://www.555-1212.com/aclookup.html

- Find an area code fast at this handy site. Simply enter a city name and/or click on a state from the drop-down list menu, then click Get Area Code! If you know the area code but want to find where the code serves, type the area code in the Area Code text box and click Get Location.

National Address and ZIP+4 Browser

http://www.semaphorecorp.com/cgi/form.html

- If you need to look up a Zip Code, go to this site and enter the company name plus as much of its address as you know. The Zip Browser returns the complete, correct address, including the correct 9-digit Zip Code. Great for cleaning up old mailing lists.

Appendix C: Viruses

Introduction

- Viruses are malicious programs written to attempt some form of deliberate destruction to someone's computer. They are instructions or code that have been written to reproduce as they attach themselves to other programs without the user's knowledge. Viruses can be programmed to do anything a computer can do. Viruses are a nuisance, but if you know how they work and take the necessary precautions to deal with them, they are manageable. It is essential that you understand the natures of these programs, how they work, and how they can be disinfected. No one is exempt from viruses; strict precautions and anti-virus programs are the answer.

- Viruses are potentially destructive to one file or to an entire hard disk, whether the file or hard disk is one used in a standalone computer or in a multi-user network. Like biological viruses, computer viruses need a host, or a program, to infect. Once infection has been transferred, the viruses can spread like wildfire through the entire library of files. Like human sickness, viruses come in many different forms; some are more debilitating than others.

Origins of Viruses

- How do you get a virus? They can come from a couple of places:
  - An infected diskette
  - Downloading an infected file from a bulletin board, the Internet, or an online service
- Knowing where viruses are likely to be introduced will make you sensitive to the possibility of getting one.

240

Categories of Viruses

- Viruses come in two categories:
  - Boot Sector Viruses
  - File Viruses

- **Boot Sector Viruses** may also be called System Sector viruses because they attack the system sector. System or boot sectors contain programs that are executed when the PC is booted. System or boot sectors do not have files. The hardware reads information in the area in the bootup sections of the computer. Because these sectors are vital for PC operation, they are prime target areas for viruses.

- Two types of system sectors exist: DOS sectors and partition sectors. PCs characteristically have a DOS sector and one or more sectors created by the partitioning command, FDISK, or proprietary partitioning software. Partition sectors are commonly called Master Boot Records (MBR). Viruses that attach to these areas are seriously damaging ones.

- **File Viruses** are more commonly found. Characteristically, a file virus infects by overwriting part or all of a file.

Timing of Viruses

- Viruses come in many sizes and with various symptoms. For example, a virus may attach itself to a program immediately and begin to infect an entire hard disk. Or the virus can be written to attack at a specific time. For example, the Michelangelo virus strikes on his birthday each May.

- Some viruses are written so that they delay letting you know of their existence until they have done major damage.

Virus Symptoms

- How can you tell if you have a virus? Hopefully, you will install anti-virus software in your PC that will identify viruses and make you aware immediately upon entry to your system. Otherwise, you may experience different symptoms such as:
  - Slow processing
  - Animation or sound appearing out of nowhere
  - Unusually heavy disk activity
  - Odd changes in files
  - Unusual printer activity

Precautions

- Most viruses spread when you have booted the computer from an infected diskette. A healthy precaution here would be to boot only from the hard drive.

  - Backup all files. At least two complete backups are recommended.

  - Even new software can come with a virus; scan every diskette before use.

  - Mark all software program attributes as read only.

  - Research and update anti-virus products on an ongoing basis to have the latest protection.

  - Since there are many types of viruses, one type of anti-virus protection won't disinfect all viruses. The safest approach is to install a multiple anti-virus program library.

Index

Index